JAMESTOWN EDUCATION

D0886245

# Content Vocabulary
# Workout™

Grade
6

Mc
Graw
Hill **Glencoe**

New York, New York    Columbus, Ohio    Chicago, Illinois    Peoria, Illinois    Woodland Hills, California

 **Glencoe**

Send all inquiries to:
Glencoe/McGraw-Hill
8787 Orion Place
Columbus, OH 43240-4027

ISBN-13: 978-0-07-874595-9 (Student Edition)
ISBN-10: 0-07-874595-0 (Student Edition)
ISBN-13: 978-0-07-874759-5 (Teacher Edition)
ISBN-10: 0-07-874759-7 (Teacher Edition)

Printed in the United States of America.

1 2 3 4 5 6 7 8 9 024 10 09 08 07 06

# Contents

# Science

# Contents

**Math**

# Contents

# To the Student

This book will help you to learn vocabulary words from Science, Math, and Social Studies. Three parts to each lesson make a lesson "workout."

 ## Vocabulary Stretches

On this page, you "stretch out" by reading about five vocabulary terms. Your teacher may have you play a game with the new words.

 ## Vocabulary Workout

In this part of the lesson, you read a selection that uses the vocabulary words. You also use the vocabulary words in an activity.

 ## Vocabulary Cooldown

In the last part of each lesson, you review the vocabulary by doing a puzzle. Here you also score the different parts of the lesson when your teacher gives you the answers.

## Assessment

After every five lessons, there is an assessment. You show what you know and get a score from your teacher.

## Scoring

You can record all your scores on page 133. That way, you can track your own progress.

Enjoy the workout!

# Science

## ⇒ Vocabulary Stretches

▶ **Read about the science words below.**

**science** *(sī´əns)* noun
**Science** is a school subject.
Science is a way of learning about the natural world.
Science also includes facts about the natural world.

**Earth science** *(urth´ sī´əns)* noun + noun
**Earth science** is a field of science.
Earth science is the study of *Earth systems*.
An *Earth system* is made of things that are not alive.
Earth science also includes the study of other planets.

**physical science** *(fiz´ikəl sī´əns)* noun + noun
**Physical science** is a field of science.
Physical science is the study of *matter* and *energy*.
*Matter* is anything that takes up space and has weight (on Earth).
An example of *energy* is the sun's rays.

**life science** *(līf´ sī´əns)* noun + noun
**Life science** is a field of science. Life science is the study of *living systems*.
A *living system* includes living things, where they live, and how they live together.

**scientific theory** *(sī´ən tif´ik thē´ər ē)* adjective + noun
A **scientific theory** is an explanation.
A scientific theory explains how or why something happens in the natural world.
A scientific theory has been tested over time by scientists.

The fields of **Earth science,**
**physical science,** and
**life science** are all related
to our planet.

▶ **"Listen" to the conversation between Luis and his teacher.**

# Choices, Choices!

"I want to study **science** in college," Luis told his teacher. "I like to find out why things happen."

Ms. Delgado said, "Great. What interests you most? Do you want to learn why elephants are disappearing? That's part of **life science,** the study of living systems."

Luis said, "Well, I do like animals."

"Maybe you're interested in earthquakes," Ms. Delgado said. "Maybe someday you'll come up with a **scientific theory** that helps predict earthquakes."

Luis smiled and said, "I could help Mexico and California!"

"That's true! The study of earthquakes is part of **Earth science,**" she explained. "What else do you want to know?"

Luis thought for a minute. "I've always wondered how DVDs work," he said. "How can a piece of plastic turn into a movie?"

"That's part of **physical science**—the study of matter and energy."

"Well," said Luis, "Then I'll study all three types of science!"

 # Vocabulary Workout

▶ **Fill in the blanks in Luis's diary. Use words from the word bank.**

**Word Bank**
science
life science
Earth science
physical science
scientific theory

Dear Diary,

I want to be a scientist! Ms. Delgado told me about the

different types of _____ I can study. One

type of science explains things like why a ball rolls downhill.

This type of science is called _____.

Another type of science is about things like how germs affect people.

It is called _____. Or I could study

_____ and learn about things like

rocks and oceans and volcanoes.

I want to study all three types of science! I'm good at asking

questions. Ms. Delgado says that asking questions is important. She

says that even the best scientists start with questions. Then they think

of ideas for answers. They collect and study information to see if

their ideas work. Then they ask more questions. Finally, they form a

_____.

I think being a scientist is for me.

_____ Workout Score (number of correct answers)

# Vocabulary Cooldown

▶ **Read the words in the word bank. Then find the words in the puzzle and circle them. Words can go up, down, across, or diagonally.**

| n | a | r | u | i | v | a | l | p | n | t | o |
| t | o | p | l | o | o | i | t | h | y | l | o |
| v | i | v | d | l | m | n | t | y | r | p | a |
| E | i | v | b | l | E | l | t | s | o | p | g |
| n | a | r | u | i | l | a | l | i | e | t | o |
| v | i | r | a | l | i | n | t | c | h | p | i |
| n | a | r | t | i | f | a | l | a | t | t | o |
| o | p | l | o | h | e | t | o | l | c | o | l |
| u | i | i | a | l | s | t | b | s | i | p | v |
| p | i | v | a | l | c | c | t | c | f | p | t |
| t | a | r | d | i | i | a | i | i | i | t | b |
| u | E | v | t | l | e | n | t | e | t | p | i |
| n | a | r | u | i | n | a | l | n | n | t | f |
| o | p | l | o | o | c | t | o | c | e | c | l |
| u | i | s | c | i | e | n | c | e | i | p | e |
| p | i | v | a | l | h | n | t | o | c | p | i |
| t | a | r | u | i | v | t | l | a | s | t | E |

**Word Bank**

science
life science
Earth science
physical science
scientific theory

_____ Workout Score (number of correct answers, p. 3)

_____ Cooldown Score (number of correct answers, this page)

☐ Add the two numbers for your Lesson 1 score.

**Write the total score on page 133 next to "Lesson 1."**

# Vocabulary Stretches

▶ **Read about the science words below.**

**infer** *(in fur´)* verb
To **infer** means to guess.
You infer using what you see or already know.

**hypothesis** *(hī poth´ə sis)* noun
A **hypothesis** is an explanation.
It explains something that happens in the natural world.
Scientists test a hypothesis to see how well it works.

**controlled experiment** *(kən trōld´ iks per´ə ment´)* adjective + noun
A **controlled experiment** is a way to test a hypothesis.
In a controlled experiment, scientists do the same test several times.
They change one part of the experiment each time to see what happens.

**constant** *(kon´stənt)* noun
The part you don't change in an experiment is the **constant.**
A controlled experiment always has at least one constant.
A constant doesn't change when the test is repeated.

**variable** *(vār´ē ə bəl)* noun
The part you change in an experiment is the **variable.**
A controlled experiment always has as least one variable.
A variable changes when the test is repeated.

Science helps us ask questions and look for answers. Have you ever wondered what a worm eats?

# Vocabulary Workout

▶ **Read about Lisa's experiment.**

## Lisa's Experiment

Lisa did her first **controlled experiment** at age 11. She found some worms after it rained. She wanted to know what they liked to eat. Lisa gathered worms and soil. Her mom gave her a big bowl and some fruit.

Lisa's **hypothesis** was that worms like apples the best. To test it, she put soil and 12 worms in the bowl. She put apple peels, banana peels, and orange peels on top of the soil. The **constants** in her experiment were the soil, the bowl, and the type of worm. The **variable** was the type of peels.

Lisa watered the soil and checked the worms every day. However, even after a week, none of the fruit peels were eaten at all! Lisa asked her mom, "Was my experiment set up right? Is fruit a food that worms EVER eat? Did being in the bowl make the worms stop eating?" Lisa could not **infer** anything from the results! Her mom said she was a good scientist, because she was still asking questions. They decided to go to the library to look for some answers.

# Vocabulary Workout

▶ **Help Emily choose the right words for her e-mail. Underline the correct word in each pair of parentheses.**

TO:     Dad

FROM: Emily

Hi, Dad! Today in class, we did an experiment. Our teacher brought a boiled egg, a boiled potato, and some french fries. We wanted to see which one has the most fat. We rubbed each one on a piece of a brown paper bag. We let the paper dry. Some foods made a more oily stain on the paper than others. Our teacher said we could (variable, infer) that a more oily stain means more fat. Our experiment was a (controlled experiment, hypothesis) because we changed only one thing each time. The type of paper bag was a (variable, constant) in the experiment because it did not change. The type of food we tested was the (variable, constant). It changed each time we did the experiment.

My (controlled experiment, hypothesis) was that the french fries had the most fat. The french fries made the most oily stain. So I can infer that my hypothesis was correct! Maybe I will be a scientist like Mom!

_____ Workout Score (number of correct answers)

# Vocabulary Cooldown

**Unscramble the letters to form the words in the word bank. Put only one letter in each box.**

1. f i n r e

   ☐☐☐☐☐

2. t a n t o n c s

   ☐☐☐☐☐☐☐☐

3. b a r v i a l e

   ☐☐☐☐☐☐☐☐

4. s e h s i t y o h p

   ☐☐☐☐☐☐☐☐☐☐

5. l o r t d e l n o c   m i r t e n p e x e

   ☐☐☐☐☐☐☐☐☐☐   ☐☐☐☐☐☐☐☐☐☐☐

**Word Bank**
hypothesis
constant
variable
infer
controlled
  experiment

_____ Workout Score (number of correct answers, p. 7)

_____ Cooldown Score (number of correct answers, this page)

☐ Add the two numbers for your Lesson 2 score.

Write the total score on page 133 next to "Lesson 2."

Vocabulary Stretches

▶ **Read about the science words below.**

**data** *(dā´tə, da´tə)* noun
**Data** is information gathered in an experiment.
Data can be words or numbers.

**measurement** *(mezh´ər mənt)* noun
A **measurement** is a number.
The number tells the size or amount of what you measure.
When you *measure* something, the result is called a measurement.

**estimate** *(es´tə mət)* noun or *(es´tə māt´)* verb
An **estimate** [noun] is a guess.
You **estimate** [verb] when you make a guess using what you already know.
You estimate when you don't have a real measurement.

**accuracy** *(ak´yər ə sē)* noun
The **accuracy** of a measurement is how close it is to the real size or amount.
If a vase is really 16 inches tall, a measurement of 15 inches is more *accurate*
than a measurement of 14 inches.

**precision** *(pri sizh´ən)* noun
**Precision** is how close you can make a measurement.
A ruler marked off in eighths of an inch is not as *precise* as a ruler
marked off in sixteenths.

On the next page, read about a
scientist from Mexico who warned
the world about spray cans.

# Vocabulary Workout

▶ **Read about scientist Mario Molina.**

## Key Players Encyclopedia

### Mario Molina, Nobel Prize Winner

Mario Molina was born in Mexico City in 1943. He studied science and learned about certain chemicals called CFCs. These chemicals are found in spray cans. Molina's hypothesis was that CFCs caused harmful pollution once they got in the air.

**Mario Molina**

Molina could not just make **estimates** to prove his ideas. He had to collect lots of **data.** He began his **measurement** of CFCs in the air by collecting air samples. The **precision** of the instruments he used helped him measure tiny differences. He did many experiments to make the **accuracy** of his data greater.

Molina's studies showed that CFCs did cause pollution. They destroy the *ozone* in the air. Ozone helps protect people from the sun's rays. Because of Molina's study, CFCs are not used anymore. In 1995, Molina won the Nobel Prize in chemistry for his work.*

*The Nobel Prize is one of the highest honors in the world. The prize was founded by Alfred Nobel, a Swedish scientist. Every year, one person gets a prize in each of six areas: chemistry, physics, medicine, peace, literature, and economics.

# Vocabulary Workout

**Help a pet shop owner write an ad. Underline the correct word in each pair of parentheses.**

Back to Nature Pet Care

1235 Main St.

Science Town, USA

At Back to Nature Pet Care, we believe in nature. We use no chemicals to treat your pets! Our shampoos are all natural. Our hair sprays for pets have no CFCs in them.

We also believe in science. We take every (measurement, precision) with only the best instruments. We use scales that weigh to the nearest gram because we value (estimates, precision)! We never mix up your pet's chart with another pet's chart because we value (estimates, accuracy)! The (precision, data) we collect on your pet is kept safely in our computer.

Finally, we believe in honesty. Before you come in, we give you an (accuracy, estimate) of the cost of the visit. We explain your pet's needs completely.

Bring your pet to Back to Nature Pet Care. Your pet will thank you!

_____ Workout Score (number of correct answers)

# Vocabulary Cooldown

▶ **Use the word bank to find the best word for each clue. Then write the words in the puzzle.**

**ACROSS**

3. A guess when you don't know exactly

5. A way to find out the length of something

**DOWN**

1. An important quality for a scientific instrument

2. A type of information

4. An important quality for a science book

_____ Workout Score (number of correct answers, p. 11)

_____ Cooldown Score (number of correct answers, this page)

[ ] Add the two numbers for your Lesson 3 score.

Write the total score on page 133 next to "Lesson 3."

# Vocabulary Stretches

## ▶ Read about the science words below.

**matter** *(mat′ər)* noun
**Matter** is any material that takes up space and has *mass*.
The mass of an object is a measurement of the amount of "stuff" in it.
(See Lesson 5 for more about mass.)

**atom** *(at′əm)* noun
The **atom** is the main "building block" of matter. It is too small to see.
There are different kinds of atoms.
One kind of atom is an iron atom.

**nucleus** *(noo′klē əs)* noun
The **nucleus** is the heavy core of an atom.

**element** *(el′ə mənt)* noun
The basic kinds of matter are called **elements.**
There is one element for each kind of atom.
Each element is made of many atoms, all of the same kind.
You can't create an element, destroy it, or turn it into something else.
An example of an element is iron.

**states of matter** *(stāts′ əv mat′ər)* noun + preposition + noun
The **states of matter** are the forms matter can be in.
There are three main states of matter.
The *solid* state is one state of matter. Matter in this state is called *a solid.*
The *liquid* state is another state of matter. Matter in this state is called *a liquid.*
The *gaseous* or gaslike state is another state of matter. Matter in this state is called *a gas.*

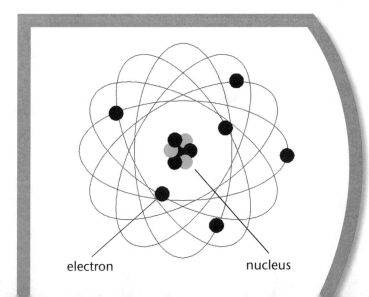

electron                    nucleus

**Diagram of an Atom**
The atom is called the "building block" of matter. However, the atom itself is made of even smaller "building blocks." The **nucleus** of an atom is in the center. Tiny particles called *electrons* go around and around the nucleus. The lines in this sketch show the paths of the electrons.

▶ **Read this ad for a movie.**

# MATTER!

This is a movie about **matter.** It is about material that takes up space in your world. *MATTER!* stars the **element** iron in the solid state. It stars the element mercury in a liquid state. And in her first movie appearance, the element oxygen is gaseous! These three famous elements show us the *solid, liquid,* and *gaseous* states. All three **states of matter** in one movie!

Then *MATTER!* takes you even deeper. Computer cartoons let you go "inside" a bar of iron to "see" its building block, the **atom.** You'll go to the heart of an iron atom and "see" the **nucleus** in the center.

If you ever wondered about the matter around you, this is a story you will never forget!

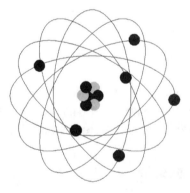

# Vocabulary Workout

▶ **Read the titles at the top of the columns. Then read the terms in the list. Place each term in the best column.**

atom          nucleus          states of matter
matter        element

| Things the Human Eye Can't See | Things the Human Eye Can Sometimes See |
|---|---|
|  |  |
|  |  |
|  |  |

▶ **Write a sentence of your own for each word or term in the word bank. The sentences do not need to be related.**

**Word Bank**
element
matter
states of matter
nucleus
atom

_____

_____

_____

_____

_____

_____

_____

_____

_____

_____

_____

_____ Workout Score (number of correct answers, from columns only)

# Vocabulary Cooldown

▶ **Read the words in the word bank. Then find them in the puzzle and circle them. Words can go up, down, across, or diagonally.**

| t | i | t | o | p | l | o | v | i | t | o | p | n | o | r |
|---|---|---|---|---|---|---|---|---|---|---|---|---|---|---|
| n | s | v | i | v | d | l | m | n | t | o | u | p | i | d |
| c | q | t | i | v | b | l | e | l | t | c | r | p | d | c |
| b | i | m | a | t | t | e | r | a | l | e | n | t | o | m |
| w | q | v | i | t | a | l | q | e | t | o | r | p | r | c |
| b | i | n | a | r | e | i | u | a | l | d | n | t | o | r |
| i | m | o | p | l | o | s | i | t | e | p | l | o | l | z |
| u | l | u | i | b | d | l | o | t | l | o | r | p | a | w |
| e | q | p | i | v | a | l | e | f | e | o | r | p | i | x |
| b | i | t | a | t | o | m | v | a | m | h | n | t | o | p |
| z | f | u | a | v | t | l | y | n | e | a | r | p | i | c |
| b | i | n | a | r | u | i | v | a | n | v | t | t | o | n |
| i | t | o | p | l | o | o | i | t | t | p | l | t | l | r |
| r | q | u | i | s | b | i | d | p | t | o | r | p | e | c |
| e | q | p | i | v | a | l | h | n | t | o | r | p | i | r |

**Word Bank**

atom
element
nucleus
matter
states of matter

_____ Workout Score (number of correct answers, p. 15)

_____ Cooldown Score (number of correct answers, this page)

[ ] Add the two numbers for your Lesson 4 score.

Write the total score on page 133 next to "Lesson 4."

# Vocabulary Stretches

▶ **Read about the science words below.**

**mass** *(mas)* noun
The **mass** of an object is the amount of "stuff," or *matter,* in it.
The mass of an object is expressed as a number and a *unit* of mass.
For example, the mass of an object could be 5 *kilograms.*

**weight** *(wāt)* noun
How much do you *weigh?* The answer is your **weight.**
The weight of an object tells how *heavy* it is.
The weight of an object is how hard gravity pulls on it.
Weight is expressed as a number and a unit of weight.
For example, an object could weigh 4.2 pounds.

**the SI** *(thē es´ī´)* article + noun
**The SI** is a system of measurement. The SI uses standard units of measure
such as the *kilogram* and the *meter* (see below).
The letters SI stand for "international system" in French.
People also call the SI the *metric system.* In the United States, the official
system of measurement is called the U.S. Customary System. It is different
from the metric system.

**kilogram** *(kil´ə gram´)* noun
A **kilogram** is a unit of mass. The kilogram is the basic mass unit in the SI.

**meter** *(mēt´ər)* noun
A **meter** is a unit of length. The meter is the basic unit of length in the SI.

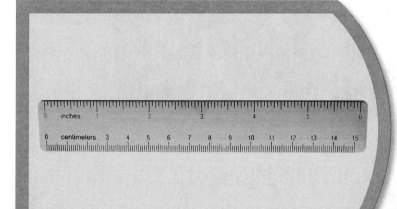

An inch is a unit of length in
the U.S. Customary System. A
centimeter is a unit of length in
**the SI.** This ruler shows both
inches and centimeters.

# Vocabulary Workout

**Read the postcard from Rita.**

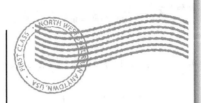

Dear Loretta,

*Hola* from Morelos, Mexico! I am having fun here with my cousins. Things are different here!

My height at home is 5 feet 3 inches, but here it is 1.6 **meters.** No, I haven't shrunk! In Mexico people use **the SI.** People in many other countries use the SI, too. The SI is a system of measurement. It is different from our system in the U.S. It has different units of measure.

As you know, my **weight** is 120 pounds in the U.S. Here they say my weight is 54.5 **kilograms!** The SI uses the unit kilogram for weight and **mass.** In the market here, people measure meat, fruit, and other foods in kilograms.

I bought you a woven shirt. Clothing sizes are different here, too. But you and I are the same size, any way you measure it. If it fits me, it will fit you!

Love,
Rita

Loretta Jones

347 Main Street

Our Town, USA

# Vocabulary Workout

**Help Loretta write a letter back to Rita. Underline the correct word in each pair of parentheses.**

Dear Rita,

I don't know much about the measurement system called (weight, the SI). Using the (kilogram, meter) instead of the pound to tell your weight is new to me. Here in the United States, a scale tells me my (meter, weight) in pounds. You say your height is only one (meter, mass) plus a little bit more. That number sounds too small! So that means one meter must be pretty big. I want to learn the math for changing from one system to the other. I hope I can visit Mexico too!

I'm glad your (kilogram, mass) hasn't changed. Otherwise I might not recognize you! They say our mass is always the same, even on the moon. But there our weight would be a lot less. We would almost float! Can you see the moon (la luna) from there?

Love,

Loretta

_____ Workout Score (number of correct answers)

# Vocabulary Cooldown

▶ **Use the word bank to find the best word for each clue. Then write the words in the puzzle.**

**ACROSS**

**2.** This is measured in pounds or kilograms

**4.** A unit of length used in the SI

**5.** The amount of matter in something

**DOWN**

**1.** A unit of mass used in the SI

**3.** The system of measurement used in Guatemala

**Word Bank**
The SI
weight
mass
kilogram
meter

_____ Workout Score (number of correct answers, p. 19)

_____ Cooldown Score (number of correct answers, this page)

[     ] Add the two numbers for your Lesson 5 score.

Write the total score on page 133 next to "Lesson 5."

▶ **Fill in the blanks with the words in the word bank.**

**Word Bank**
weight
meter
mass
The SI
kilogram

**The Birth of the SI**

_____ is an international system of measurement. The system was created in Paris in 1875. Many countries signed an agreement. They created *units* of measurement that would always be the same. They created a unit for length. They called this unit the _____. The unit for _____ was named the _____. This unit is also used to tell the _____ of an object. Most countries now use the SI, which is also called the *metric system*.

▶ **Underline the correct words to help Kathleen write in her science notebook.**

I saw a movie in class today. I learned that (matter, nucleus) is all the "stuff" that makes up the world. Matter is made of millions of (states of matter, atoms). They are so tiny that we can't even see them. Still each one has a center part, or (element, nucleus). The movie showed a huge piece of iron. Iron is made of only one kind of atom. Iron is an (element, atom). The iron got red hot and melted! It went through two (elements, states of matter), solid and liquid.

# Lessons 1–5 Assessment

▶ **Read the titles at the top of the columns. Then read the terms in the list. Place each term in the best column.**

scientific theory      infer      precision      hypothesis
controlled experiment    estimate    measurement    accuracy

| Words About Finding and Giving Explanations | Words About Describing Size or Amount |
|---|---|
| | |
| | |
| | |
| | |

▶ **Write a sentence of your own for each word or term in the list. The sentences do not need to be related.**

science      life science      Earth science      physical science
constant      variable      data

_____

_____

_____

_____

_____

_____

_____

_____

_____

# Science

## Vocabulary Stretches

▶ **Read about the science words below.**

**mineral** *(min´ər əl)* noun
A **mineral** is a solid material. It is not alive.
The atoms of a mineral are always in the same pattern.
A mineral is found in nature. An example of a mineral is quartz crystal.

**rock** *(rok)* noun
A **rock** is a solid material. A rock is not alive.
A rock usually has two or more minerals in it.

**gem** *(jem)* noun
A **gem** is a rare mineral. A gem is valuable because it is beautiful.
An example of a gem is a diamond.
People cut and polish gems to use in jewelry.

**ore** *(ôr)* noun
**Ore** is a type of rock.
Ore may contain metals like copper and gold.
Miners drill for ore. The metals in ore can be sold.

**sedimentary rock** *(sed´ə men´tər ē rok´)* adjective + noun
**Sedimentary rock** is one type of rock.
Sedimentary rock has different layers.
The layers form over long periods of time.
The layers have different kinds of minerals and rocks.

The Yuba River in Arizona contains **ore.**

# Vocabulary Workout

## Trip to a Gold Miner's Ghost Town!

Some people call Downieville, California a ghost town. Do you dare to visit? Take our tour and learn about Charlie Wilkins and Albert Callis, two of the first African American miners. They founded Downieville. They settled there because they found gold in the Yuba River in 1849. They used pans to sort through sand and **rocks** from the river bottom. Some of the rocks were **ore.** The ore had metals in it, including gold. Around 1865, most of the gold ran out. Almost everyone left Downieville. Except the ghosts!

**Panning for gold**

You may not see any ghosts on this trip. However, you will see the beautiful cliffs of **sedimentary rock** along the Yuba River. Each layer of rock is a different color. You can wade into the river and try "panning" for gold! We supply the pans. On past trips, people have found **minerals** such as a quartz crystal. Who knows, you might even find a **gem** for jewelry!

# Vocabulary Workout

▶ **Fill in the blanks in Katara's postcard. Use words from the word bank.**

**Word Bank**
mineral
ore
gem
rock
sedimentary rock

Dear Granny Callis,

Hi from California! This ghost town is really cool. Do you know if our family is related to Albert Callis? He was one of the people who founded the town.

The land is different here. The cliffs have layers of

_____. The Yuba River contains

_____ with gold and other metals. Ore

is one type of _____. You can also find

_____ such as quartz in rocks. Most

of all, I want to find a beautiful _____

such as a diamond. However, that almost never happens.

See you when we get home. I'm having a great time!

Love,

Katara

347 Main Street

Hometown, USA

_____ Workout Score (number of correct answers)

# Vocabulary Cooldown

▶ **Unscramble the letters to form the words in the word bank. Put only one letter in each box.**

**1.** e g m

☐☐☐

**2.** r o e

☐☐☐

**3.** k o c r

☐☐☐☐

**4.** r i m n e l a

☐☐☐☐☐☐☐

**5.** t e n m i d e s r a y   c o k r

☐☐☐☐☐☐☐☐☐☐☐   ☐☐☐☐

_____ Workout Score (number of correct answers, p. 25)

_____ Cooldown Score (number of correct answers, this page)

☐ Add the two numbers for your Lesson 6 score.

Write the total score on page 133 next to "Lesson 6."

# Vocabulary Stretches

▶ **Read about the science words below.**

**crust** *(krust)* noun
The **crust** is the outer layer of Earth.

**fault** *(fôlt)* noun
In Earth science, a **fault** is a line in the crust of Earth.
A fault can be many miles long.
A fault forms when giant layers of Earth "slip" partway past each other.

**plate** *(plāt)* noun
In Earth science, a **plate** is part of the crust of Earth.
A plate is a giant sheet of rock.
The plates of Earth are as big as continents.

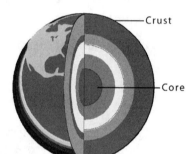

**core** *(kôr)* noun
The **core** is the center of Earth.
The core is made of a solid metal center.
There is hot, liquid metal around the core.

**volcano** *(vol kān´ō)* noun
A **volcano** is a place where melted rock comes out
  from below Earth's surface.
When the melted rock sprays out, we say the volcano *erupts*.
The melted rock it is called *lava*. The lava cools and forms rock.
Over time, the lava builds up and forms a mountain.
Volcanoes usually form along faults in Earth's surface.

The Colima Volcano is the most active **volcano** in Mexico. In this picture, the volcano is erupting.

# Vocabulary Workout

▶ **Read the want ad.**

**Help Wanted:** Students to work for scientists on a **volcano**

**Place:** Base camp on El Chichón, a volcano in Mexico

**Job:** Collect soil and rocks made of lava for experiments. Travel to other volcanoes along the major **fault.** Help senior scientists measure movements of Earth near the fault. Go to nearby schools to teach students about volcanoes in Spanish.

**You must be able to:**

- Speak Spanish. Measure and record data in Spanish.
- Explain **plate** movements of Earth to students. Draw map of major volcanoes of Mexico along the fault line.
- Explain the difference between the **crust** of Earth and the **core** to students.

**Education:** High school diploma. Excellent grades in Science.

**Write to:** Dr. Rafael Ochoa

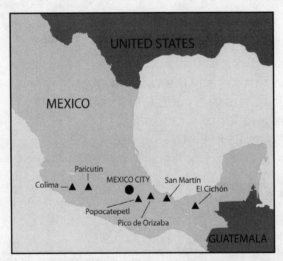

**Major Volcanoes of Mexico**

 **Vocabulary Workout**

▶ **Fill in the blanks in Socorro's answer to Dr. Ochoa's ad. Use words from the word bank.**

**Word Bank**
volcano
fault
crust
plate
core

Dear Dr. Ochoa:

I am applying for the job on El Chichón.

I graduated from high school in June. My Science Fair project was a model of Earth. It showed the outer layer, or _____. It also showed the _____ in the center. I labeled each _____ of Earth's surface. I showed that when two huge layers of rock move against each other, a _____ forms. I also showed that along faults there are always volcanoes and earthquakes.

I am fluent in Spanish. My grandparents live near El Chichón. They still remember March 28, 1982. That day the _____ erupted. Many people were killed.

I want to become a scientist. I want to help predict when volcanoes will erupt. That way I can save lives. The job on El Chichón is my first step.

Sincerely,

Socorro Vallejo

_____ Workout Score (number of correct answers)

# Vocabulary Cooldown

▶ **Unscramble the letters to form the words in the word bank. Put only one letter in each box.**

1. s u r t c

   ⬜⬜⬜⬜⬜

2. t e p a l

   ⬜⬜⬜⬜⬜

3. l u t a f

   ⬜⬜⬜⬜⬜

4. r o e c

   ⬜⬜⬜⬜

5. n a o c l o v

   ⬜⬜⬜⬜⬜⬜⬜

**Word Bank**
fault
crust
core
plate
volcano

_____ Workout Score (number of correct answers, p. 29)

_____ Cooldown Score (number of correct answers, this page)

⬜ Add the two numbers for your Lesson 7 score.

Write the total score on page 133 next to "Lesson 7."

# Vocabulary Stretches

▶ **Read about the science words below.**

**humidity** *(hū mid´ə tē)* noun
**Humidity** is the amount of *water vapor* in the air.
*Water vapor* is water in a gaseous state.

**weather** *(weth´ər)* noun
**Weather** is the current condition of the air around a place.
The temperature and humidity of the air are part of the weather.
The amount of rainfall and the speed of the wind are also part of
 the weather.

**tornado** *(tôr nā´dō)* noun
A **tornado** is a violent, whirling wind shaped like a funnel.
A tornado travels over land and sometimes touches the ground.

**hurricane** *(hur´ə kān´)* noun
A **hurricane** is a huge storm.
A hurricane forms over an ocean.
Hurricanes have extremely fast, powerful winds.
They bring heavy rains, thunder, lightning, and flooding.

**precipitation** *(pre sip´ə ta´shən)* noun
**Precipitation** is the formation of raindrops, hailstones,
 or snowflakes in the sky.
The rain, snow, or hailstones are also called precipitation.
Precipitation can also be freezing rain, called *sleet*.

A **tornado** such as this one can lift
an entire house. The wind speed
can be over 200 miles per hour.

# Vocabulary Workout

▶ **Read the newspaper article about Hurricane Katrina.**

## Katrina Rips Into New Orleans

August 29, 2005. This morning a giant **hurricane** named Katrina ripped into the city of New Orleans. It formed over the ocean and came inland. The speed of the wind is now over 150 miles per hour. The city expects 20 inches of **precipitation** and waves up to 25 feet high.

New Orleans is by the ocean. The **weather** in New Orleans always depends on the conditions at sea. The **humidity** in the air is high. People expect storms, starting in the spring. But they have never known a storm like Katrina. Thousands of people are taking shelter in the Superdome. Visitors from Kansas commented, "This is worse than any **tornado** we've ever seen." Parts of the city may soon be under 30 feet of water. Aid from other parts of the country is already coming in.

A building loses its roof during **Hurricane** Katrina.

# Vocabulary Workout

▶ **Read the titles at the top of the columns. Then read the terms in the list. Place each term in the best column.**

weather          hurricane          tornado
humidity         precipitation

| There Is Always Rain With These Things | There Is Not Always Rain With These Things |
|---|---|
|  |  |
|  |  |
|  |  |
|  |  |

▶ **Write a sentence of your own for each word or term in the word bank. The sentences do not need to be related.**

**Word Bank**
hurricane
weather
humidity
precipitation
tornado

_____
_____
_____
_____
_____
_____
_____
_____
_____
_____

_____ Workout Score (number of correct answers, from columns only)

# Vocabulary Cooldown

▶ **Use the word bank to find the best word for each clue. Then write the words in the puzzle.**

**ACROSS**

3. Drops of water or ice that fall from clouds

4. The amount of water vapor in the air

5. A huge storm that forms over an ocean

**DOWN**

1. A violent, whirling wind

2. The current condition of the air around a place

**Word Bank**

hurricane
weather
humidity
precipitation
tornado

_____ Workout Score (number of correct answers, p. 33)

_____ Cooldown Score (number of correct answers, this page)

[    ] Add the two numbers for your Lesson 8 score.

Write the total score on page 133 next to "Lesson 8."

## Vocabulary Stretches

▶ **Read about the science words below.**

**comet** *(kom´it)* noun
A **comet** is a large body of ice, rock, dust, and gas.
A comet moves in an orbit around the sun.
When a comet nears the sun, it develops a bright, burning tail.

**galaxy** *(gal´ək sē)* noun
A **galaxy** is a huge group of stars, gas, dust, and other materials.
Many galaxies make up the universe.
The Earth belongs to the galaxy called the Milky Way.

**meteorite** *(mē´tē ə rīt´)* noun
A **meteorite** is a piece of rock from space.
A meteorite falls from space and hits Earth.
Meteorites are mostly made of iron and stone.

**constellation** *(kon´stə lā´shən)* noun
A **constellation** is a group of stars.
A long time ago, people gave names to constellations.
They imagined "connecting the dots" between stars to make a figure.
The name of each constellation is the name of the figure they imagined.
Some constellations are the Big Bear, the Horse, and the Big Dipper.

**solar system** *(sō´lər sis´təm)* adjective + noun
The **solar system** includes planets and other objects that orbit a star, called its sun.
The Earth is in a solar system of planets that orbit our star, called the Sun.

**Halley's Comet**
On the next page, read about the man who first saw this comet.

# Vocabulary Workout

▶ **Read this article about a famous comet.**

## Halley's Comet

Edmund Halley was an English scientist born in 1656. He helped people understand what they saw in the sky. Hundreds of years ago, people knew that the Sun and the planets formed a group. However, they did not know that the Sun was at the center of the **solar system.** People saw that a **constellation** "stayed" in one place. They saw that a comet moved across the night sky with a tail of light. People knew that a **meteorite** could hit Earth. But they didn't know that all these things are part of a **galaxy** of stars.

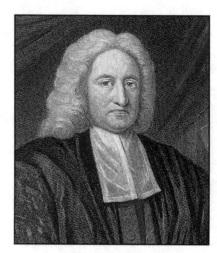

**Edmund Halley**

One year, Halley saw a **comet.** It looked like a bright light moving across the sky. He read history books to find data about comets. He found that a bright comet was seen in 1531, 1607, and 1682. That's about every 76 years! Halley thought it was the same one he had seen. His hypothesis was that comets go around the Sun in an orbit. Every time they come around, they can be seen on Earth. Halley used math to figure out that "his" comet would be seen on Earth every 76.1 years. He was right! The comet is now known as "Halley's comet." It is expected to be near Earth's orbit again in 2062. Maybe you will see it! You will be approximately 70 years old.

# Vocabulary Workout

▶ **Help a museum director write a sign about this photograph. Underline one word in each pair.**

**Halley's Comet**

A (comet, galaxy) is made from ice, rock, dust, and gas. It has

a burning tail. Comets are one kind of object in the Milky Way,

which is our (meteorite, galaxy). Halley's comet travels through

our (constellation, solar system) near Earth every 76.1 years.

When we look at a star in a pattern, or (constellation, comet),

it seems to stay still among the other stars in the group. But a

comet moves quickly across the sky. Usually, comets do not hit

Earth. But a smaller (meteorite, constellation) from a comet's tail

can fall to Earth.

Halley's comet will appear again around 2062.

_____ Workout Score (number of correct answers)

# Vocabulary Cooldown

▶ **Read the words in the word bank. Then find the words in the puzzle and circle them. Words can go up, down, across, or diagonally.**

| m | i | n | a | r | u | i | v | a | l | e | n | t | b | o |
|---|---|---|---|---|---|---|---|---|---|---|---|---|---|---|
| d | g | t | m | e | t | e | o | r | i | t | e | l | n | y |
| a | r | v | i | v | d | l | m | n | t | o | r | p | i | r |
| c | q | u | i | v | b | l | s | l | t | o | r | p | s | c |
| m | i | n | g | r | h | e | o | r | m | e | d | t | o | w |
| w | q | v | i | m | a | l | l | n | t | o | r | p | i | c |
| b | i | n | a | r | u | g | a | l | a | x | y | t | s | g |
| i | t | o | p | l | o | o | r | t | o | p | l | o | w | r |
| u | l | u | i | i | r | m | s | t | b | o | r | p | k | p |
| e | q | p | i | v | a | l | y | n | t | o | g | p | i | s |
| b | i | t | a | r | u | i | s | a | l | h | n | t | e | f |
| z | f | u | a | v | t | n | t | d | c | o | r | p | i | c |
| b | i | n | a | r | u | i | e | o | l | v | n | t | m | u |
| i | t | m | p | l | o | t | m | t | o | p | l | o | c | r |
| r | q | u | i | s | r | e | t | p | t | o | r | p | i | c |
| e | c | o | n | s | t | e | l | l | a | t | i | o | n | t |
| b | i | t | a | r | u | i | v | q | l | a | u | t | e | d |

**Word Bank**

galaxy
solar system
comet
constellation
meteorite

_____ Workout Score (number of correct answers, p. 37)

_____ Cooldown Score (number of correct answers, this page)

[   ] Add the two numbers for your Lesson 9 score.

Write the total score on page 133 next to "Lesson 9."

# Vocabulary Stretches

▶ **Read about the science words below.**

**orbit** *(ôr´bit)*  noun or verb
An **orbit** is a path around a star or planet.
To orbit means to go around and around, or *circle,* a star or planet.

**rocket** *(rok´it)*  noun
A **rocket** is an engine.
A rocket can push spaceships through space.

**satellite** *(sat´əl īt´)*  noun
A **satellite** is an object that orbits a larger object in space.
The Moon is a satellite of Earth. Man-made satellites are used for
communication or navigation. They also orbit Earth.

**space shuttle** *(spās´ shut´əl)*  noun + noun
A **space shuttle** is a spaceship.
It carries people, supplies, and equipment from Earth into space.
A space shuttle returns to Earth.
Space shuttles can make many trips to space and back to Earth.

**space station** *(spās´ sta´shən)*  noun
A **space station** is like a building that "floats" in space.
A space station follows an orbit around Earth.
A space shuttle can travel to a space station to pick up or drop
off astronauts.
Astronauts live and work in a space station. They do experiments
there to learn more about space.

**The U.S. International Space Station**

# Vocabulary Workout

▶ **Read the e-mail to James from Brenda.**

TO:      James
FROM:  Brenda

James! I just met an amazing woman named Lybrease Woodard. I was at the Marshall Space Flight Center in Huntsville, Alabama. The Flight Center is run by NASA, the government organization that made the **space shuttle.**

Ms. Woodard has been in charge of experiments done on the space shuttle. She has also been in charge of experiments on the **space station.** The space station is in **orbit** around Earth.

Here is a picture of Ms. Woodard at work.

Ms. Woodard showed me a life-size model of a **rocket** that shot a **satellite** into space. It was so big. You could almost feel the power of the rocket just standing next to it. The satellite is orbiting Earth and taking pictures of it right now! You have to come visit this place.

**Lybrease Woodard (right) at work**

Brenda

# Vocabulary Workout

▶ **Complete the Venn diagram below using words from the following list.**

orbit
satellite

infer (from Lesson 2)
space station

estimate (from Lesson 3)

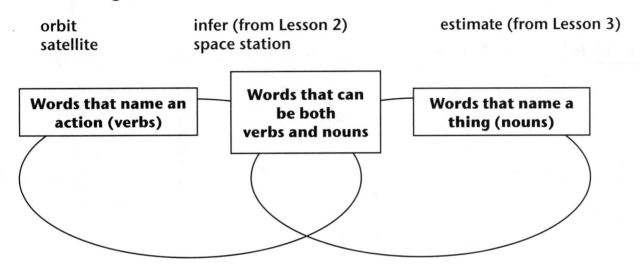

Words that name an action (verbs)

Words that can be both verbs and nouns

Words that name a thing (nouns)

▶ **Write a sentence of your own for each word. The sentences do not need to be related.**

**Word Bank**
orbit
rocket
satellite
space station
space shuttle

_____

_____

_____

_____

_____

_____

_____

_____

_____

_____

_____ Workout Score (number of correct answers, from Venn diagram only)

# Vocabulary Cooldown

▶ **Read the words in the word bank. Then find them in the puzzle and circle them. Words can go up, down, across, or diagonally.**

| o | i | t | o | p | l | o | o | i | t | o | p | l | o | r |
|---|---|---|---|---|---|---|---|---|---|---|---|---|---|---|
| a | q | v | i | v | d | l | m | s | t | o | r | p | i | v |
| c | q | u | i | v | b | l | e | p | t | o | r | p | i | m |
| s | s | p | a | c | e | s | t | a | t | i | o | n | o | y |
| w | q | v | i | m | a | l | q | c | t | o | r | p | i | c |
| b | r | n | a | r | u | i | v | e | l | d | n | t | o | o |
| i | o | o | p | l | o | o | i | s | o | p | l | o | r | r |
| u | c | u | i | s | a | l | e | h | b | o | r | b | i | b |
| e | k | p | i | v | a | l | e | u | t | o | i | p | i | x |
| b | e | t | a | r | u | t | v | t | l | t | n | t | o | y |
| z | t | u | a | v | t | l | e | t | t | o | r | p | i | c |
| b | i | n | a | r | u | i | v | l | l | v | n | t | o | z |
| i | t | o | p | l | o | d | i | e | l | p | l | o | l | r |
| r | q | u | i | s | b | i | t | p | t | i | r | p | i | q |
| e | q | p | i | v | a | p | h | n | t | o | t | p | i | c |
| b | i | t | a | b | u | i | v | d | g | a | u | e | e | m |
| a | q | h | q | i | c | z | w | b | e | y | n | t | c | g |
| q | d | t | a | r | h | m | v | a | p | a | n | b | b | y |

**Word Bank**
orbit
rocket
satellite
space station
space shuttle

_____ Workout Score (number of correct answers, p. 41)

_____ Cooldown Score (number of correct answers, this page)

[   ] Add the two numbers for your Lesson 10 score.

**Write the total score on page 133 next to "Lesson 10."**

▶ **Underline the correct word in each set of parentheses.**

Dear Diary,

I saw the Big Dipper tonight. It looks like a giant spoon in the sky. It is my favorite (constellation, galaxy). I wonder if I will ever see a (solar system, comet) burning across the sky. I also wonder if anyone has ever seen a (meteorite, constellation) right before it hit Earth. When I looked up at the sky, I imagined all the planets in our (solar system, meteorite). Then I imagined all those planets and all those stars as part of our huge (galaxy, comet). I felt small. But right now my pillow looks big to me!

▶ **Read the e-mail. Then fill in the blanks with the words in the box.**

TO:        Jen
FROM:      Lin
SUBJECT:   School in space!
DATE:      September 1, 2050

**Word Bank**
satellite
space station
rocket
orbit
space shuttle

Hi, Jen. I'm writing you from space! I'm traveling on the

_____ called *Discovery Learning*.

I can see a huge _____ that burns fuel right

outside my window. It is pushing us through space. Inside the ship, there are cool

ramps everywhere. My wheelchair can roll right down them. Elevators take me back up!

I can't believe they chose ME to attend the first school in space. The school is on a

_____ that floats in space. Well, it doesn't exactly float.

It goes around Earth in an _____. That means I am going to school on

a _____ of Earth!

▶ **Read the titles at the top of the columns. Then read the terms in the list. Place each term in the best column.**

| weather | fault | humidity | rock | mineral |
|---|---|---|---|---|
| hurricane | tornado | plate | precipitation | |

| Things That Are in the Crust of the Earth | Things That Happen in the Air |
|---|---|
| | |
| | |
| | |
| | |
| | |

▶ **Write a sentence of your own for each word or term in the list. The sentences do not need to be related.**

| gem | ore | sedimentary rock |
|---|---|---|
| core | volcano | crust |

---

# Vocabulary Stretches

▶ **Read about the math words below.**

**data** *(dā´tə, da´tə)* noun
Measurements and other facts are **data.**
People record data in experiments, calculations, and other activities.
Data can be words or numbers.
Your name and address, your age, and your favorite foods are all data.

**survey** *(sur´vā)* noun
A **survey** has at least one question. A survey is usually a list of questions.
You give a survey to people to collect information.

**statistics** *(stə tis´tiks)* noun
**Statistics** are a collection of data.
Sports fans like to read the statistics of great players.
There is also a field of mathematics called *statistics.*

**graph** *(graf)* noun
A **graph** is a picture.
A graph presents data as a picture.

**bar graph** *(bär´ graf´)* noun + noun
A **bar graph** is a type of graph. A bar graph uses thick bars.
The length of the bars represents the data.

A young Michael Jordan makes a slam dunk. On the next page, read some of Jordan's **statistics.**

# Vocabulary Workout

▶ **Read the article and bar graph below.**

## Michael Jordan Still a Favorite

In 1993, a group called Harris Interactive® took a **survey** of people across the country. The question on the survey was, "Who is your favorite sports star?" The number-one answer was basketball player Michael Jordan. Harris took the same survey every year from 1995 to 1999 and from 2003 to 2005. Jordan won every year!

Why is he still a favorite? Besides his personal charm, Jordan has great **statistics.** In basketball, one kind of statistics is number of points scored. The **bar graph** below shows the points Jordan scored over 13 seasons. This **graph** doesn't give the **data** in exact numbers. It gives the data in a picture. You can easily see, for example, that Jordan scored above the 2,500 line in six different seasons! One reason Michael Jordan is still a favorite is that his statistics are so good.

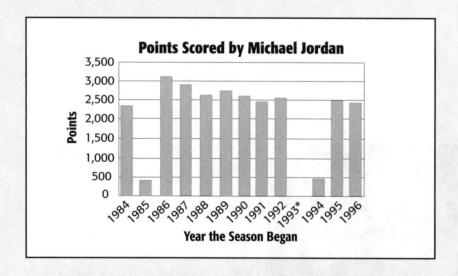

\* In 1993, Michael Jordan did not play professional basketball.

# Vocabulary Workout

▶ **Fill in the blanks to help Jody write a letter to her Aunt Fan, who is a big fan of Michael Jordan. Use words from the word bank.**

**Word Bank**
survey
bar graph
statistics
data
graph

Dear Aunt Fan,

Harris Interactive® took a _____ over several years. The question was, "Who is your favorite sports star?" Michael Jordan won every year!

I saw a _____, which is one type of graph, about the points Michael Jordan scored. The bars on this _____ showed _____, or information. Most of the bars were near the 2,500 line. That means Michael scored about 2,500 points almost every year! I would like to see the rest of Michael's _____ in graphs. I know you are a fan of Michael Jordan. Do you have any other graphs about his statistics?

Sincerely,

Jody

_____ Workout Score (number of correct answers)

# Vocabulary Cooldown

▶ **Use the word bank to find the best word for each clue. Then write the words in the puzzle.**

**ACROSS**

4. A collection of data, as in basketball
5. A picture that uses bars to show data

**DOWN**

1. A type of information
2. In general, a picture that shows data
3. A question or list of questions

**Word Bank**
graph
bar graph
statistics
data
survey

_____ Workout Score (number of correct answers, p. 47)

_____ Cooldown Score (number of correct answers, this page)

[   ] Add the two numbers for your Lesson 11 score.

**Write the total score on page 133 next to "Lesson 11."**

 ## Vocabulary Stretches

▶ **Read about the math words below.**

**number system** *(num´bər sis´təm)* noun + noun
*Numbers* are symbols. Numbers tell how many or how much.
A **number system** is a method, or set of rules.
A number system tell us how to write the numbers.

**digit** *(di´jət)* noun
A **digit** is a number from 0 to 9.
In our number system, we use digits to write larger numbers.
The digits of a number are like the letters of a word.

**place-value system** *(plās´ val´ū sis´təm)* adjective + noun
A **place-value system** is one type of number system.
In a place-value system, the value of a digit depends on its place.
For example, the numbers 10, 100, and 101 have different values because
   the digits 1 and 0 are in different places.

**base-ten system** *(bās´ ten´ sis´təm)* adjective + noun
The **base-ten system** is one type of place-value system.
The base-ten system uses ten digits, 0 through 9.
In the base-ten system, the number 10 has a value of 1 ten and 0 ones.

**base-two system** *(bās´ tōō´ sis´təm)* adjective + noun
The **base-two system** is another type of place-value system.
The base-two system uses only two digits, 0 and 1.
In the base-two system, the number 10 has a value of 1 two and 0 ones.

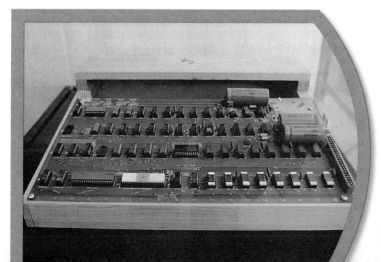

The first Apple computer used a
code in the **base-two system.**
Computers today still use the
base-two system.

# Vocabulary Workout

▶ **Read the true story below. Then read an imaginary letter about an alphabet code that uses the base-two system.**

## Making Codes

In 1963, Steve Wozniak was in 6th grade. That year, he made a simple computer. He wrote a code so the computer could play tic-tac-toe. Computer codes use a **place-value system** called a **base-two system.** This system has only two **digits,** 1 and 0. (Our regular **number system** is a **base-ten system.** It has ten digits, 0 through 9.) Later, Wozniak and his friend Steve Jobs used the base-two system to make the first home computer. They formed a company called Apple Computers.

Dear Sung-Joo,

I made up an alphabet code. We can use it to send secret messages. The code gives a number for each letter of the alphabet. But the numbers are in the base-two system! No one will ever figure out this code. Here is the rule:

| | | | |
|---|---|---|---|
| A= 1 | J= 1 0 1 0 | S= 1 0 0 1 1 |
| B= 1 0 | K= 1 0 1 1 | T= 1 0 1 0 0 |
| C= 1 1 | L= 1 1 0 0 | U= 1 0 1 0 1 |
| D= 1 0 0 | M= 1 1 0 1 | V= 1 0 1 1 0 |
| E= 1 0 1 | N= 1 1 1 0 | W= 1 0 1 1 1 |
| F= 1 1 0 | O= 1 1 1 1 | X= 1 1 0 0 0 |
| G= 1 1 1 | P= 1 0 0 0 0 | Y= 1 1 0 0 1 |
| H= 1 0 0 0 | Q= 1 0 0 0 1 | Z= 1 1 0 1 0 |
| I= 1 0 0 1 | R= 1 0 0 1 0 | |

Here's a test message:

MEET ME AT 5 PM AT:     101-1100-1101    1-1110-100   1101-1-1001-1110.

Your friend,

Marisol

# Vocabulary Workout

▶ **Help Sung-Joo answer Marisol's letter. Underline the correct word in each pair of parentheses.**

December 9, 2005

Dear Marisol,

I think I understand the rule for your code. It's in the way you write the numbers. Our regular number system is the (base-ten system, base-two system). But your code uses a different (digit, number system). It's called the (base-two system, base-ten system), right? You use only ones and zeroes as the (digits, base-ten system). The value of a 1 depends on its place. So the base-two system is a (place-value system, digit). I think we could do a lot more with this code!

I figured out your message. I'll meet you at Elm and Main at 5 p.m.

Sung-Joo

_____ Workout Score (number of correct answers)

# Vocabulary Cooldown

▶ **Unscramble the letters below to form the words in the word bank. Put only one letter in each box.**

1. i i t g d

   ☐☐☐☐☐

**Word Bank**
digit
place-value system
number system
base-two system
base-ten system

2. b r u m e n  e s m y t s

   ☐☐☐☐☐☐  ☐☐☐☐☐☐

3. e l p a c - e l v a u  m y s t e s

   ☐☐☐☐☐☐  ☐☐☐☐☐  ☐☐☐☐☐☐

4. s a b e - o w t  t y e s s m

   ☐☐☐☐☐  ☐☐☐  ☐☐☐☐☐☐

5. e s b a - e n t  m e y s t s

   ☐☐☐☐☐  ☐☐☐  ☐☐☐☐☐☐

_____ Workout Score (number of correct answers, p. 51)

_____ Cooldown Score (number of correct answers, this page)

☐ Add the two numbers for your Lesson 12 score.

Write the total score on page 133 next to "Lesson 12."

## Vocabulary Stretches

▶ **Read about the math words below.**

**fraction** *(frak´shən)* noun
  A **fraction** is a number like ¼.
  The bottom number tells how large the parts of the whole are.
  The top number tells how many parts you have.

**denominator** *(di nom´ə nā´tər)* noun
  The bottom number in a fraction is the **denominator.**
  The denominator tells the *size* of the parts of the whole.

**numerator** *(noo´mə rā´tər)* noun
  The top number in a fraction is the **numerator**.
  The numerator tells *how many* parts make the value of the fraction.

**equivalent fractions** *(i kwi´və lənt frak´shəns)* adjective + noun
  The word *equivalent* means *equal.*
  Some fractions have equal value but they are written differently.
  They are called **equivalent fractions.**
  Examples of equivalent fractions are ½ and ³⁄₆.
  They have equal value, but they are written differently.

**mixed number** *(mikst´ num´bər)* adjective + noun
  A **mixed number** is a whole number with a fraction.
  An example of a mixed number is 2¾.

1/3    1/9

7 1/4

5

2 1/2

28

Which of these numbers are
**mixed numbers?**

# Vocabulary Workout

**"Listen" to Leticia's telephone conversation with Denise.**

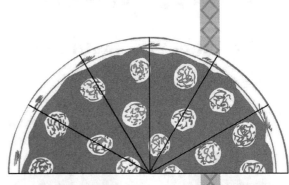
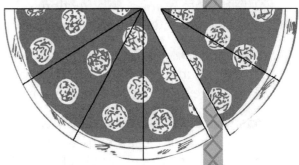

LETICIA: Hello?

DENISE: Hi, it's Denise. Sorry I missed your pizza party.

LETICIA: That's okay.

DENISE: Tanya told me that Derrick ate half a pizza by himself.

LETICIA: No. Each pizza had 12 pieces. Derrick ate 4 pieces. That's not half.

DENISE: More like a fourth?

LETICIA: Well, the whole pizza had 12 pieces. So 12 is the **denominator.** The part Derrick ate, 4, is the **numerator.** So he ate $\frac{4}{12}$ of the pizza. His **fraction** of the pizza was $\frac{4}{12}$.

DENISE: Girl, you're on fire!

LETICIA: An **equivalent fraction** of $\frac{4}{12}$ is $\frac{1}{3}$. So Derrick ate $\frac{1}{3}$ of the pizza.

DENISE: Wow! How many pizzas did the group eat altogether?

LETICIA: We ate 2 whole pizzas plus 1 piece from the third pizza.

DENISE: That's 2 and $\frac{1}{12}$ pizzas.

LETICIA: Hey, you're good with **mixed numbers.**

DENISE: Thanks. Where are the 11 pieces that were left over?

LETICIA: Here on my table. Want to come over?

DENISE: Great! I'll be right there. I can beat Derrick's record!

# Vocabulary Workout

▶ **R**ead the titles at the top of the columns. Then read the terms in the list. Place each term in the best column.

fraction
equivalent fractions

denominator
mixed number

numerator

| Whole Numbers | Not Always Whole Numbers |
|---|---|
|  |  |
|  |  |
|  |  |

▶ **W**rite a sentence of your own for each word or term in the word bank. The sentences do not need to be related.

_____

_____

_____

_____

_____

_____

_____

_____

_____

_____

_____

_____

_____ Workout Score (number of correct answers, from columns only)

# Vocabulary Cooldown

▶ **Read the words in the word bank. Then find them in the puzzle and circle them. Words can go up, down, across, or diagonally.**

| f | i | n | a | q | u | b | m | a | n | x | o | t | e | y |
|---|---|---|---|---|---|---|---|---|---|---|---|---|---|---|
| r | i | t | o | p | i | t | o | u | q | m | p | l | q | r |
| a | q | v | i | v | d | e | m | u | d | b | r | p | u | d |
| c | q | u | f | v | b | l | s | l | d | o | h | p | i | t |
| b | i | n | a | r | u | v | a | l | e | n | t | f | v | e |
| w | q | v | i | e | a | l | q | n | n | o | m | p | a | c |
| b | i | n | r | t | u | c | v | a | l | a | n | t | l | m |
| i | t | o | e | l | o | o | t | i | c | p | l | o | e | r |
| u | l | z | b | i | a | l | e | i | b | o | r | p | n | e |
| e | t | p | m | b | a | q | o | n | o | o | r | p | t | s |
| b | f | t | u | q | u | pi | v | a | t | n | o | t | f | y |
| z | r | u | n | v | t | w | y | a | t | o | t | p | r | m |
| b | a | r | d | e | u | z | n | a | l | v | a | t | a | k |
| i | c | o | e | l | o | x | i | t | o | p | r | o | c | r |
| r | t | u | x | s | m | r | t | p | t | o | e | p | t | d |
| e | i | u | i | o | a | l | o | n | t | o | m | p | i | c |
| b | o | t | m | r | u | d | v | a | l | a | u | t | o | q |
| a | n | e | g | k | s | a | t | d | m | h | n | s | n | m |
| q | s | d | e | n | o | m | i | n | a | t | o | r | s | y |

**Word Bank**

mixed number
numerator
fraction
equivalent
  fractions
denominator

---

_____ Workout Score (number of correct answers, p. 55)

_____ Cooldown Score (number of correct answers, this page)

[    ] Add the two numbers for your Lesson 13 score.

**Write the total score on page 133 next to "Lesson 13."**

# Vocabulary Stretches

▶ **Read about the math words below.**

**area** *(ãr´ē ə)* noun
The **area** is the size of a flat surface.
You write an area in square units, such as "square inches."
A card that is 3 inches by 5 inches has an area of 15 square inches.

**perimeter** *(pə rim´ə tər)* noun
**Perimeter** is the distance around the outside edge of a flat surface.
The perimeter is also the outside edge itself.

**right angle** *(rīt´ ang´gəl)* adjective + noun
An *angle* is formed by two lines that start at the same point.
A **right angle** is a kind of angle.
The two lines of a right angle make a square corner.

**Right angle**

**two-dimensional** *(too´ di men´shən əl)* adjective
A **two-dimensional** object has only two *dimensions,* length and width.
The length of a tablecloth is how long it is. The width is how wide it is.
A two-dimensional object is flat. It does not have height or thickness.
A graph is two-dimensional.

**three-dimensional** *(thrē´ di men´shən əl)* adjective
A **three-dimensional** object has three *dimensions.*
It has *length, width,* and *height.*
The height of a cake is how high or how tall it is.

This drawing is called *Relativity.* On the next page, you will read about the artist who drew it. The drawing looks **three-dimensional** and almost real. However, when you look at it, you can't tell what's up!

# Vocabulary Workout

▶ **Read the article about M.C. Escher.**

## Math in Art

M.C. Escher, a Dutch artist, was born in 1898. Escher loved math. He used math to create interesting patterns in his drawings. He went beyond flat squares and **right angles.** He was able to imagine and draw things that would not be possible in real life.

One of Escher's drawings is called *Reptiles.* The drawing is **two-dimensional.** When you touch it, it feels flat. The **area** of a paper is its length times its width. However, it looks **three-dimensional!** The reptiles in the drawing seem to be on top of the paper. Then they melt back into it. The reptiles look flat and two-dimensional again.

*Reptiles*

Each of the "flat" reptiles fits partly inside the **perimeter** of a 5-sided shape. You can see the same shape on the large three-dimensional solid in the middle of the drawing.

# Vocabulary Workout

▶ **Write a letter to a friend about the drawings *Reptiles* and *Relativity*. Underline the correct word or phrase in each pair of parentheses.**

Dear _____,

    I am sending you some cool pictures. Look at the first picture called Reptiles. The artist drew lizards in two ways. He made them flat, or (three-dimensional, two-dimensional) in the center. Then as they walk around the picture, they start to look (three-dimensional, two-dimensional). As the lizards come back to the center, they look flat again. Do you see what I mean?

    Now look at the second picture. It is called *Relativity*. The stairs by themselves look normal. The sides of the steps form (area, right angles) with each other. However, you can't measure the (area, right angles) of the floor because you can't tell where the floor is. You can't find the (perimeter, area) of the room because you can't go all the way around it. Escher calls the drawing *Relativity* because "up" and "down" are *relative* to (related to) the part of the drawing you are looking at. What do you think?

Sincerely,

_____
(your name)

_____ Workout Score (number of correct answers)

# Vocabulary Cooldown

▶ **Unscramble the letters below to form the words in the word bank. Put only one letter in each box.**

1. r i g t h   l e g n a

|   |   |   |   |   |   |

|   |   |   |   |   |   |

2. e e e i r p m t r

|   |   |   |   |   |   |   |   |   |

3. e a a r

|   |   |   |   |

4. h e e t r - s i l n i a o e m d n

|   |   |   |   |   |   |

|   |   |   |   |   |   |   |   |   |   |   |

5. o w t - i i a o e d m n s n l

|   |   |   |

|   |   |   |   |   |   |   |   |   |   |   |

_____ Workout Score (number of correct answers, p. 59)

_____ Cooldown Score (number of correct answers, this page)

|   | Add the two numbers for your Lesson 14 score.

Write the total score on page 133 next to "Lesson 14."

# Vocabulary Stretches

▶ **Read about the math words below.**

**vertex** *(vur´teks)* noun
A **vertex** is a point where straight lines of a figure meet.
More than one vertex are called vertices.
A square has four vertices. A triangle has three vertices.

**polygon** *(pol´ē gon´)* noun
A **polygon** is a closed two-dimensional figure.
A polygon has three or more lines as sides.
A square, a triangle, and a pentagon (5 sides) are polygons.

**pyramid** *(pir´ə mid´)* noun
A **pyramid** is a three-dimensional figure. It is a solid figure.
A pyramid is made of triangles joined at their edges.
The triangles meet at the top at a vertex, or point.
The pyramid also has a base at the bottom.

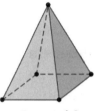

**Pyramid**

**edge** *(ej)* noun
An **edge** is a straight line like a line we draw with a pencil.
An edge is the boundary between two flat surfaces.
Edges are found on solid figures. For example, they are
  found on cubes and pyramids.

**prism** *(priz´əm)* noun
A **prism** is a solid figure. It has two bases.
The bases of the prism are polygons.
The two polygons are exactly the same.

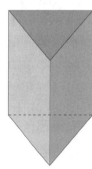

**Prism**

On the next page, read about the
man who designed the Visual Arts
Center in Santa Fe, Arizona. He
used **polygons, pyramids** and
even a **prism.**

# Vocabulary Workout

▶ **Read about Ricardo Legorreta.**

## Key Players Encyclopedia

### Making Buildings with Math

Ricardo Legorreta learned math in Mexico, where he grew up and went to college. He became an *architect.* He uses math to design buildings. Legorreta has designed buildings in many countries. People like the strong, beautiful colors he uses. He first saw these colors in Mexican art. He also uses shapes and figures from ancient buildings such as Mayan **pyramids.**

**Ricardo Legorreta**

The Visual Arts Center in Santa Fe, Arizona was designed by Legorreta. The building has a tower in the shape of a **prism.** Legorreta also put three pyramids on top of the building. In the photo on page 61, you can see how the **edges** of each triangle meet at the **vertex** at the top. The other sides of the building look like different **polygons.**

Like the Mayas before him, Legorreta makes buildings with math.

 **Vocabulary Workout**

▶ **Read the titles at the top of the columns. Then read the terms in the list. Place each term in the best column.**

edge        prism        polygon
vertex     pyramid

| A Point | A Line | Two-dimensional | Three-dimensional |
|---------|--------|-----------------|-------------------|
|         |        |                 |                   |
|         |        |                 |                   |

▶ **Write a sentence of your own for each word in the word bank. The sentences do not need to be related.**

**Word Bank**
pyramid
edge
polygon
prism
vertex

_____

_____

_____

_____

_____

_____

_____

_____

_____

_____

_____

_____ Workout Score (number of correct answers, from columns only)

# Vocabulary Cooldown

▶ **Read the words in the word bank. Then find them in the puzzle and circle them. Words can go up, down, across, or diagonally.**

| i | i | o | p | l | o | t | e | p | o | l | y | g | r | q |
|---|---|---|---|---|---|---|---|---|---|---|---|---|---|---|
| o | m | d | r | p | l | o | x | i | t | o | p | l | o | p |
| e | q | p | i | v | d | l | e | n | t | o | r | p | w | c |
| z | d | u | s | m | i | l | y | m | s | i | r | p | s | t |
| b | i | g | a | r | m | i | v | a | l | v | n | t | b | e |
| i | t | o | e | p | a | e | e | t | o | p | l | o | x | r |
| r | q | u | i | s | r | i | d | p | s | o | h | n | s | i |
| e | g | e | i | t | y | m | p | n | t | l | r | p | d | s |
| a | q | v | e | r | p | i | r | d | e | y | y | r | g | m |
| c | q | x | i | v | b | s | e | l | t | g | r | d | m | g |
| b | i | n | a | s | u | m | s | a | x | o | n | t | o | b |
| w | q | v | i | m | a | l | t | n | t | n | r | p | d | c |
| b | i | n | a | p | u | d | v | g | r | e | n | t | j | d |
| p | o | l | y | b | o | n | g | d | e | p | l | q | w | r |
| u | l | s | i | i | a | l | g | e | v | d | r | p | t | m |
| b | i | p | a | s | u | i | s | m | l | p | u | d | e | x |

**Word Bank**

vertex
edge
prism
pyramid
polygon

_____ Workout Score (number of correct answers, p. 63)

_____ Cooldown Score (number of correct answers, this page)

☐ Add the two numbers for your Lesson 15 score.

**Write the total score on page 133 next to "Lesson 15."**

# Lessons 11–15 Assessment

▶ **Read Aunt Fan's answer to Jody's question about Michael Jordan. Underline the word that completes each sentence.**

Jody,

Guess what! Harris Interactive® is taking another (survey, bar graph) about favorite sports stars! I hope Michael Jordan wins again. Also, I found Michael's (graph, statistics) on free throws. The (data, survey) is one large number. He made a total of 7,327 free throws! There is a chart with more data at www.nba.com. Why don't you use the information in the chart to make your own (statistics, graph)? It can show total free throws by different players. Make it a (data, bar graph) by using one bar for each player!

Sincerely, Aunt Fan

Jody Hunter

123 Main St.

Fantown, USA

▶ **Read the imaginary letter from Steve Wozniak. Then fill in the blanks with the words in the list.**

**Word Bank**
place-value system
digits
base-two system
number system
base-ten system

Dear Carlos,

I made a computer! To make the code, I used a _____

with only two digits. That place-value system is called the

_____. The only _____ are 1 and 0. The

base-two system is a good _____ for computers. Electric signal in different

parts of a computer can be either on or off. "On" means 1 and "off" means 0. I send all the

instructions and information to the computer in ones and zeroes! A number system with more

choices for digits, such as the _____, is not necessary.

Steve

# Lessons 11–15 Assessment

▶ **Read the titles at the top of the columns. Then read the terms in the list. Place each term in the best column.**

denominator          numerator          polygon          fraction
mixed number         prism              pyramid          right angles

| Solid Things | Flat Things | Numbers |
|---|---|---|
|  |  |  |
|  |  |  |
|  |  |  |
|  |  |  |

▶ **Write a sentence of your own for each word or term in the list. The sentences do not need to be related.**

perimeter          area                    vertex
edge               equivalent fraction

| |
|---|
| _____ |
| _____ |
| _____ |
| _____ |
| _____ |
| _____ |
| _____ |
| _____ |
| _____ |
| _____ |

# ⊜ Vocabulary Stretches

▶ **Read about the math words below.**

**sum** *(sum)* noun
A **sum** is a number. When you add numbers, the result is the sum.
The sum of a group of numbers is also called their total.

**difference** *(dif´ər əns)* noun
A **difference** is a number.
When you subtract numbers, the result is the difference.
The difference of two numbers tells how much larger one is.

**place value** *(plās´ val´ū)* noun + noun
In a place-value system, each **place** in a number has a **value.**
Examples of **place values** are hundreds, tens, ones, tenths, and hundredths.
In the number 23, the digit 2 is in the tens place. The value of the 2 is really 20.
The 3 is in the ones place. The value of the 3 is 3.

**decimal system** *(des´ə məl sis´təm)* noun + noun
The **decimal system** is a number system.
A *decimal number* has a dot called a *decimal point.*
The digits to the *left* of the decimal point name a whole number.
The digits to the *right* of the decimal point name a number smaller than 1.
In the number 4.5, the 4 means 4 ones. The 5 means 5/10.

**round** *(round)* verb
When you **round** a *decimal number,* you get a new number.
The new number is called a *round number.* The *round number* is easier to work with.
To round a number, you first choose a place value. You round *to that place value.*
If you round 17.6 *to the nearest one,* the round number is 18.
If you round 17.6 *to the nearest ten,* the round number is 20.

We write amounts of money
using the **decimal system.**

$24.35   $31.16
    $10.35

# Vocabulary Workout

▶ **Read the article about jobs in math.**

## Jobs in Math: Rounded Numbers

The table below shows jobs in math. It also shows about how much a person could make per hour in 2003 at each job.

Dollar amounts are written in the **decimal system,** so it is easy to **round** them. First, we pick a **place value.** Look at the first five dollar amounts in the table below. Let's round to the nearest ten-dollar bill (the tens place). The round amounts are $20, $30, $10, $10, and $40 per hour. Now let's round to the nearest one-dollar bill (the ones place). The round amounts are $24, $31, $10, $13, and $40 per hour. The second list is closer to the real values. That is, the **difference** between those round numbers and the real values is smaller.

Now, let's say you get one of the math jobs below AND marry someone who has another math job! The money you would make together would be the **sum** of the two amounts per hour.

| Job | Money Made Per Hour (average)* |
|---|---|
| Accountant | $24.35 |
| Architect | $31.16 |
| Bank Teller | $10.35 |
| Billing Clerk | $12.79 |
| College Math Teacher | $39.78 |
| Computer Scientist | $33.26 |
| Economist | $31.37 |
| Finance Manager | $42.05 |
| Mechanical Engineer | $31.65 |
| Statistician | $28.56 |

*Source: National Compensation Survey, July 2003

# Vocabulary Workout

▶ **Help the Math Department chairperson write this memo. Underline the correct word in each set of parentheses.**

TO:      Dr. Susan Wood, Principal, Brown High School

FROM:  Debbie Jones, Chairperson, Math Department

RE:      Jobs in Math

Let's have a math job fair! Some jobs in math pay $30 or $40 per hour, when you (round, place value) to the nearest $10. For someone who makes $8 per hour now, that's a (difference, sum) of $22 to $32 per hour.

My student Bernard could get a job in math. He did a great project on the (decimal system, round). He brought a box with four drawers in a row. The one farthest on the left was for $10 bills. It had a (place value, decimal system) of 10. The next three drawers were for $1 bills, dimes, and pennies. Students counted how many bills or coins were in each drawer: 3, 4, 8, 2. Bernard wrote a 3 on the tens drawer, a 4 on the ones drawer, an 8 on the dimes drawer, and a 2 on the pennies drawer. Next, Bernard took out all the money and added it up. The (difference, sum) of all the bills and coins was $34.82.  The digits in the decimal number were the same as the numbers on the drawers! Bernard explained that the decimal system works like his system of drawers.

I think students like Bernard would be interested in a math job fair.

_____ Workout Score (number of correct answers)

# Vocabulary Cooldown

▶ **Use the word bank to choose the right word for each clue. Then write the words in the puzzle.**

**ACROSS**

2. The result when you subtract one number from another

3. The number system we use to write amounts of money

5. You could do this to 12.348 to make it simpler

**DOWN**

1. The value of a place in a number

4. The result when you add two numbers

**Word Bank**

place value
difference
decimal system
sum
round

_____ Workout Score (number of correct answers, p. 69)

_____ Cooldown Score (number of correct answers, this page)

☐ Add the two numbers for your Lesson 16 score.

Write the total score on page 133 next to "Lesson 16."

## Vocabulary Stretches

▶ **Read about the math words below.**

**product** *(prod´əkt)* noun
A **product** is a number.
When you multiply two numbers, the result is the product.
The product of 4 and 3 is 12.

**quotient** *(kwō´shənt)* noun
A **quotient** is a number.
When you divide two numbers, the result is the quotient.
When you divide 10 by 2, the quotient is 5.

**percent** *(pər sent´)* noun
A **percent** is a number. The number 100% is the same as the whole number 1.
You can think of 100% as "one whole thing" or "the whole amount."
A percent less than 100%, such as 75%, means a part of the whole.

**ratio** *(rā´shē ō´)* noun
A **ratio** is a way to compare numbers. We see 3 : 1 and we say, "Three to one."
You can use a ratio to compare two groups: "The ratio of boys to girls is 3 to 1."
You can also use a ratio to compare a part to a whole: "Head length to whole body
  length is 1 to 8."

**proportion** *(prə pôr´shən)* noun
A **proportion** is a statement. "1 : 8 = 10 : 80" is a proportion.
This statement says that two ratios are equal.
If you know a proportion, you can use one ratio instead of the other.
If head length to body length is 1:8, then an 80-foot statue of a person should have
  a 10-foot head.

On the next page, read about how artist Leonardo da Vinci used **proportions** to describe the human body. This drawing by da Vinci is called *The Vitruvian Man.*

▶ **Read the article about Leonardo da Vinci.**

## Key Players Encyclopedia

### Leonardo da Vinci (1452–1519), Pioneer of Proportions

Leonardo da Vinci was an Italian who lived over 500 years ago. He studied proportions in art and science. Leonardo noticed that the length of an adult body, including the head, is about 8 times the length of the head alone. That is, the **ratio** of "head length to body length" is 1:8. So if Leonardo painted a picture with a head 10 inches long, the body had to be 80 inches long. The **proportion** says that 1:8 = 10:80.

**Leonardo da Vinci**

You can check to make sure this proportion is true. Find the **product** of the largest and smallest numbers of the proportion (1 and 80). That product is 80. 1 x 80 = 80. Then find the product of the middle numbers in the proportion (8 and 10). That product is also 80. 8 x 10 = 80. In every proportion, those two products must be equal.

Another way to express Leonardo's ratio 1:8 is to say that the length of the head is 12.5 **percent** of the length of the whole body. 12.5 percent is the answer, or **quotient,** you get when you divide 1 by 8.

# Vocabulary Workout

▶ **Read the titles at the top of the columns. Then read the terms in the list. Place each term in the best column.**

product       ratio            proportion
percent      quotient

| Numbers | Comparisons | Statements |
| --- | --- | --- |
|  |  |  |
|  |  |  |
|  |  |  |

▶ **Write a sentence of your own for each word in the word bank. The sentences do not need to be related.**

**Word Bank**
product
ratio
proportion
percent
quotient

_____

_____

_____

_____

_____

_____

_____

_____

_____

_____

_____ Workout Score (number of correct answers, from columns only)

# Vocabulary Cooldown

▶ **Read the words in the word bank. Then find them in the puzzle and circle them. Words can go up, down, across, or diagonally.**

| b | i | n | a | r | u | i | v | a | l | e | n | t | z | d |
|---|---|---|---|---|---|---|---|---|---|---|---|---|---|---|
| o | i | t | o | p | r | o | o | i | d | o | p | l | o | r |
| a | w | p | i | v | d | l | m | n | w | d | r | p | i | e |
| c | z | q | i | v | b | l | e | l | t | i | r | r | i | r |
| b | i | c | u | r | u | i | v | t | l | a | n | o | o | t |
| w | q | t | i | o | a | l | q | n | t | o | r | d | i | d |
| b | i | n | i | r | t | i | v | u | i | d | n | u | o | n |
| i | t | o | p | o | r | i | r | t | o | p | l | c | m | e |
| u | l | u | r | i | o | c | e | n | b | r | r | t | i | c |
| e | q | p | o | t | a | l | e | n | t | o | r | p | i | t |
| b | i | t | p | a | u | n | v | a | t | d | n | t | n | y |
| z | f | u | o | r | t | l | y | n | t | o | r | e | i | c |
| b | i | n | r | r | u | c | t | a | l | r | c | t | o | y |
| i | t | o | p | r | p | r | o | p | o | r | t | i | o | n |
| r | q | u | i | s | b | i | t | p | e | o | r | p | h | g |
| e | a | p | i | v | a | l | h | p | t | o | m | r | u | c |
| b | i | d | a | o | u | w | v | a | k | a | u | t | e | q |
| a | q | w | a | g | c | i | o | n | m | y | q | d | c | m |

**Word Bank**

product
quotient
percent
ratio
proportion

_____ Workout Score (number of correct answers, p. 73)

_____ Cooldown Score (number of correct answers, this page)

[  ] Add the two numbers for your Lesson 17 score.

**Write the total score on page 133 next to "Lesson 17."**

# Vocabulary Stretches

## ▶ Read about the math words below.

**actual size** *(ak´chōō əl sīz´)* adjective + noun
The **actual size** of something is its real size.
A photograph of a house cannot be actual size. It cannot be the same size as the house.

**ratio** *(rā´shē ō´)* noun
A **ratio** is a way to compare numbers. We see 3:1 and we say, "Three to one."
You can use a ratio to compare two groups: "The ratio of boys to girls is 3 to 1."
You can also use a ratio to compare a model to real life: "The ratio of the size of the toy train to the size of the real train is 1 to 87."

**scale** *(skāl)* noun
A **scale** is a ratio.
A scale compares the size of a model or picture to the actual size of the object.
A scale of 1:8 means the real thing is 8 times bigger than the model or picture.

**scale drawing** *(skāl´ drô´ing)* noun + noun
A **scale drawing** shows an object in a different size from the actual size.
The drawing is a different size, but the proportions of the object are the same.
You can find the actual size of the object if you know the scale of the drawing.

**linear measure** *(lin´ē ər mezh´ər)* adjective + noun
The distance between two points on a line is the **linear measure.**
You measure string in linear measure.
You buy string by the yard.

The **scale** of this toy train is 1:87.
The real train is 87 times bigger.

# Vocabulary Workout

▶ **Read the e-mail about toy trains.**

TO:       Kevin
FROM:    Gregoria
SUBJECT: Scales for toy trains

Hey, Kevin, what's up? I'm looking for a toy train for my brother Patrick's birthday.

Did you know that the **scale** of toy trains can be different? A scale is the **ratio** between the size of a model and the **actual size** of the train. The smallest scale for trains is the *Z* scale, which is 1:220. So if the real train has a **linear measure** of 220 feet, the model is 1 foot long.

There are other scales for toy trains, such as the *S, O,* and *N* scales. Most stores sell the *HO* scale, which is 1:87. You can see a **scale drawing** of an *HO* train on the box. The engine is 2 inches high, which is a good size for Patrick.

I'll let you know which train I get.

Gregoria

# Vocabulary Workout

▶ **Help Kevin write an e-mail back to Gregoria. Use the words in the word bank to finish it.**

**Word Bank**
scale drawing
actual size
linear measure
ratio
scale

TO:        Gregoria
FROM:      Kevin
SUBJECT:   Scales for toy trains

Hi, Gregoria. I've got an idea. Let's build a model town. We can

use the same scale as your brother's train. The train can run through our

model town.

We can pick a few buildings in our town and find out how tall they are. Then

we will know their _____. We can make models of

the buildings using the *HO* _____. The _____ of

the *HO* scale is 1:87. First we should make a _____

of each model on a piece of paper. We should also check the

_____ of the sides of the room where the train is. We

can't build a town that won't fit in the room!

Are you "on board" to do this?

Kevin

_____ Workout Score (number of correct answers)

# Vocabulary Cooldown

▶ **Unscramble the letters below to form the words in the word bank. Put only one letter in each box.**

1. i o t r a

   ☐☐☐☐☐

2. l u c t a a   z e s i

   ☐☐☐☐☐☐☐   ☐☐☐☐

3. e a l c s

   ☐☐☐☐☐

4. r i l a n e   s e e m a r u

   ☐☐☐☐☐☐   ☐☐☐☐☐☐☐

5. l e a s c   g a n i r d w

   ☐☐☐☐☐   ☐☐☐☐☐☐☐

_____ Workout Score (number of correct answers, p. 77)

_____ Cooldown Score (number of correct answers, this page)

☐ Add the two numbers for your Lesson 18 score.

Write the total score on page 133 next to "Lesson 18."

# Vocabulary Stretches

▶ **Read about the math words below.**

**measurement units** *(mezh´ər mənt  ū´nits)* noun
Some examples of **measurement units** are inches and kilograms.
Measurement units describe length, volume, and weight.
The *metric system* and the *United States* or *customary system* use different
measurement units.

**volume** *(vol´yōōm)* noun
The **volume** of an object is the amount of space the object takes up.
We measure volume in cubic units.
An example of a cubic unit is a cubic meter.

**median** *(mē´dē ən)* noun
The **median** is a number.
The median is one way to describe the center of a set of numbers.
The median is the middle of a set when the numbers are arranged in order.

**mode** *(mōd)* noun
The **mode** is a number.
The mode is one way to describe the center of a set of numbers.
The mode is the number that shows up most often in the set.

**mean** *(mēn)* noun
The **mean** is a number. The mean is one way to describe the center of a set of numbers.
Another word for mean is *average*. If you add all the values in a set, then divide by the
number of values in the set, you get the average value or mean value.

The **volume** of a swimming
pool is the amount of water that
it holds. You can measure the
amount in cubic feet or cubic
meters. The two numbers and
the **measurement units** are
different, but the volume is
the same.

# Vocabulary Workout

▶ **Read the story below.**

## Average Town

Average Town has 25 adults of working age. Here is the list of the amount of money, or *salary,* each person makes in a year:

| | | | | | |
|---|---|---|---|---|---|
| $0 | $0 | $0 | $0 | $0 | $0 |
| $0 | $0 | $0 | $0 | $0 | $0 |
| $20,000 | $20,000 | $20,000 | $20,000 | $20,000 | |
| $20,000 | $20,000 | $20,000 | $20,000 | $20,000 | |
| $50,000 | $50,000 | $4,000,000 | | | |

The mayor of Average Town found the average, or **mean,** of all the salaries. Then he made a TV commercial. It said, "Come to live in Average Town! The average salary here is $172,000!"*

The mayor was right about the mean. There are 25 salaries. If you add them together and divide by 25, you get an average of $172,000. However, he left out some information. He didn't say that the **median** salary is only $20,000. The median is the number exactly in the middle of the list. Another statistic he forgot is the **mode.** The mode is the number that shows up the most often. In Average Town, there are 12 people out of work. The most common salary is $0! To describe a set of data well, you have to tell all three statistics: the mean, the mode, and the median.

*The mayor also said the town has a pool with a **volume** of 16,000 cubic meters! He got the wrong **measurement units.** (See the next page.)

# Vocabulary Workout

**Help Terrell answer the mayor's commercial. Underline the correct word in each set of parentheses.**

Dear Mr. Mayor,

I saw your commercial about Average Town. It said that the (volume, mean) of the salaries is $172,000. However, it didn't say the median or the mode. You need all three to see the whole picture.

There is one person in Average Town, Mr. Barnes, who makes four million dollars a year. That one salary makes the mean go way up. The middle salary, or the (mode, median), is still $20,000. And the most common salary is no salary! The largest number of adults are not working at all, so the (mode, measurement units) is $0. Average Town isn't doing as well as you made it sound.

One more thing: Mr. Barnes' pool is 100 feet long, 40 feet wide, and 4 feet deep. The (volume, mode) is 16,000 cubic *feet,* not cubic meters. A cubic meter is over 27 times as big as a cubic foot. You are using the wrong (median, measurement units). Not even Mr. Barnes could have a pool that big!

Sincerely,

Terrell Bennett

_____ Workout Score (number of correct answers)

# Vocabulary Cooldown

▶ **Read the words in the word bank. Then find them in the puzzle and circle them. Words can go up, down, across, or diagonally.**

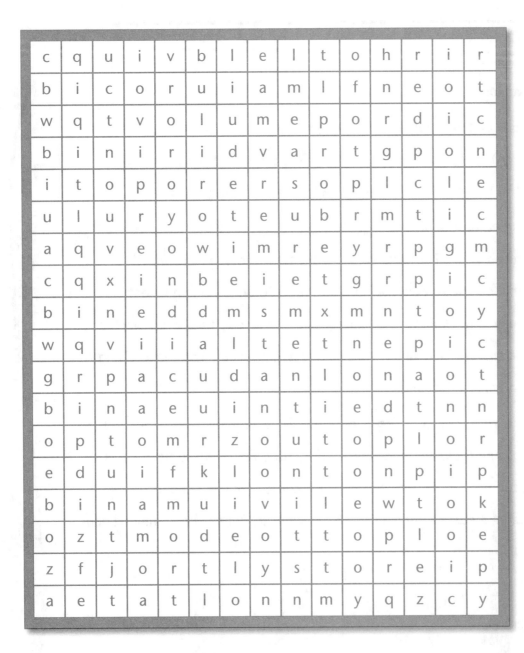

**Word Bank**
volume
mean
mode
median
measurement
 units

| c | q | u | i | v | b | l | e | l | t | o | h | r | i | r |
| b | i | c | o | r | u | i | a | m | l | f | n | e | o | t |
| w | q | t | v | o | l | u | m | e | p | o | r | d | i | c |
| b | i | n | i | r | i | d | v | a | r | t | g | p | o | n |
| i | t | o | p | o | r | e | r | s | o | p | l | c | l | e |
| u | l | u | r | y | o | t | e | u | b | r | m | t | i | c |
| a | q | v | e | o | w | i | m | r | e | y | r | p | g | m |
| c | q | x | i | n | b | e | i | e | t | g | r | p | i | c |
| b | i | n | e | d | d | m | s | m | x | m | n | t | o | y |
| w | q | v | i | i | a | l | t | e | t | n | e | p | i | c |
| g | r | p | a | c | u | d | a | n | l | o | n | a | o | t |
| b | i | n | a | e | u | i | n | t | i | e | d | t | n | n |
| o | p | t | o | m | r | z | o | u | t | o | p | l | o | r |
| e | d | u | i | f | k | l | o | n | t | o | n | p | i | p |
| b | i | n | a | m | u | i | v | i | l | e | w | t | o | k |
| o | z | t | m | o | d | e | o | t | t | o | p | l | o | e |
| z | f | j | o | r | t | l | y | s | t | o | r | e | i | p |
| a | e | t | a | t | l | o | n | n | m | y | q | z | c | y |

_____ Workout Score (number of correct answers, p. 81)

_____ Cooldown Score (number of correct answers, this page)

☐ Add the two numbers for your Lesson 19 score.

**Write the total score on page 133 next to "Lesson 19."**

## Vocabulary Stretches

▶ **Read about the math words below.**

**point** *(point)* noun
A **point** is a dot on a graph.
A point is a location where two lines cross.

**coordinate graph** *(kō ôr´də nit´ graf´)*
adjective + noun
A **coordinate graph** is a drawing on grid paper.
The line across the page is the the *x-axis.*
The line up and down the page is the *y-axis.*
A coordinate graph shows points in space
  by using those two lines.

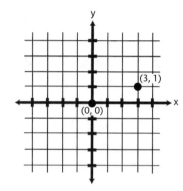

**ordered pair** *(ôr´durd pār´)* adjective + noun
An **ordered pair** is a pair of numbers, such as (3, 1).
An ordered pair names a point on a graph.
The ordered pair gives directions for how to get to the point if you start at (0, 0).
  The first number tells you how many to "move" along the x-axis. The second
  number tells you how many to move up or down.

**table** *(tā´bəl)* noun
A **table** is a drawing. A table shows data in rows and columns.
A table makes the data easier to read.

**variable** *(vār´ē ə bəl´)* noun
A **variable** is a letter of the alphabet. The letter represents a number.
A variable can be used to solve problems.
A variable can also be used to make statements in math and science.

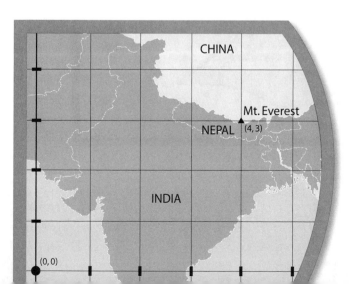

This is a map with a **coordinate graph** on it. On the next page, read about two imaginary space aliens who used this map to get to Mount Everest, the highest mountain in the world.

▶ **Read the story below.**

# The Adventures of Quap and Zreep

Quap and Zreep flew from their home planet of Skrog to Earth. They wanted to see Mount Everest because it was the highest mountain. Quap was piloting the spaceship. Zreep looked at a map of the area with a **coordinate graph** on it. He checked a **table** that showed data for the location of mountains. The table said that Mount Everest was at the **ordered pair** (4, 3). Quap knew that in any ordered pair (*x, y*), the **variable** *x* represents the number to count ACROSS the bottom of the graph. The variable *y* represents the number to count UP to find the **point.**

Quap flew their spaceship to the point (4, 3). But they were missing some information. . . .

# Vocabulary Workout

▶ **Help Quap send an emergency e-mail home. Use the words in the word bank to finish it.**

TO: Skrog

FROM: Quap

Emergency! We have crashed into a mountain!

I am sending a map with lines on it. The lines make a

_____. The _____ where we are

is labeled Mount Everest. The _____ for this

point is (4, 3). Check the information in the rows and columns of the

_____ I sent. Again, our value for the variable *x* on the map is 4.

Our value for the variable *y* is 3. Please send help!

TO: Quap

FROM: Skrog

We have your location. Help is on the way. And don't worry, we also

know the value of *z*, the _____ that tells us the height

of the mountain!

_____ Workout Score (number of correct answers)

# Vocabulary Cooldown

▶ **Use the word bank to find the best word or term for each clue. Then write the words in the puzzle.**

**ACROSS**

**3.** A drawing to show points

**5.** Columns and rows that show data

**DOWN**

**1.** (2, 3) is an example of this

**2.** A letter that stands for a number

**4.** A dot on a coordinate graph

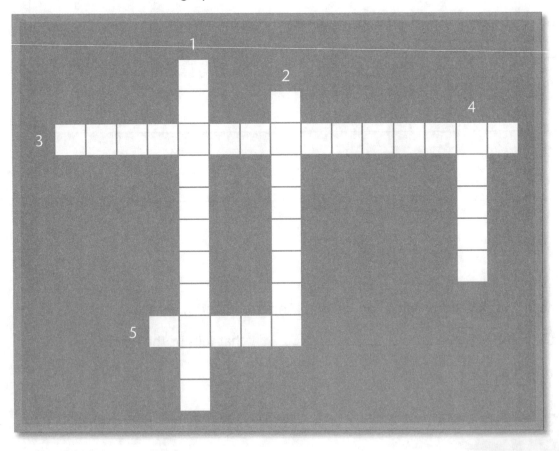

_____ Workout Score (number of correct answers, p. 85)

_____ Cooldown Score (number of correct answers, this page)

[　　　] Add the two numbers for your Lesson 20 score.

Write the total score on page 133 next to "Lesson 20."

# Lessons 16–20 Assessment

▶ **Fill in the blanks to answer the questions about the table.**

| x | y | ? |
|---|---|---|
| 2 | 6 | (2, 6) |
| 4 | 1 | (4, 1) |
| 5 | 3 | (5, 3) |

**Word Bank**
table
variable
points
ordered pair
coordinate graph

The drawing above is called a _____.

The *x* and the *y* are _____.

Where the question mark is, the title should be _____.

The ordered pairs in the table give the locations of three _____.

You can show these points on a _____.

▶ **Underline the correct word in each set of parentheses.**

**Making a Map**

   To draw a map, you have to know the (actual size, scale drawing) of

the area. However, you can't fit the whole area onto a piece of paper. So

you have to decide on a (linear measure, scale) that tells how many times

smaller your map is. Once you know the scale, you can create a (linear

measure, scale drawing). For example, your scale could have a (ratio,

actual size) of 1:1,000. Every inch on the map means 1,000 inches in real

life. The (ratio, linear measure) from one place to another on the map

shows people about how far they have to travel.

# Lessons 16–20 Assessment

▶ **Read the titles at the top of the columns. Then read the terms in the list. Place each term in the best column.**

median          difference          mode          product
quotient        mean                sum

| Words That Name a Result in Math | Words That Describe a Set of Numbers |
|---|---|
| | |
| | |
| | |
| | |

▶ **Write a sentence of your own for each word or term in the list. The sentences do not need to be related.**

place value     decimal system     round              percent
proportion      volume             measurement units  ratio

_____

_____

_____

_____

_____

_____

_____

_____

_____

# Vocabulary Stretches

▶ **Read about the social studies words related to the ancient Mayas.**

**astronomers** *(əs tron′ə mərs)* noun
**Astronomers** are scientists.
Astronomers study stars, planets, and other things in space.

**civilization** *(siv′ə li zā′ shən)* noun
A **civilization** is a developed society.
A civilization has cities, trade, art, science, and written records.
A civilization also has its own government.

**pyramid** *(pir′ə mid′)* noun
A **pyramid** is a building.
The four sides of a pyramid look like triangles.
Many years ago, some civilizations built pyramids.
The pyramids were usually holy places.

**pilgrimage** *(pil′grə mij)* noun
A **pilgrimage** is a trip to a holy place.

**ancestors** *(an′ ses′tərs)* noun
**Ancestors** are family members.
They are relatives from long ago.
Ancestors are not alive.

On the next page, read about the secret of this Mayan **pyramid** at Chichén Itzá, Mexico.

# Vocabulary Workout

▶ **Read about a giant snake made of shadows.**

## Key Players Encyclopedia

### Snake on the Pyramid!

The Mayan people built an early **civilization** in the lands that are now called Mexico, Guatemala, and Belize. The Mayas are the **ancestors** of many people living in these countries today. The ancient Mayas were experts in math. Some Mayas were **astronomers**. They wrote about the stars

In this photo, you can see the "snake" on the pyramid of Kukulcán at Chichén Itzá. The small white arrow at the lower left points to the snake's head.

and made calendars. The Mayas also made buildings called **pyramids**. The pyramid of Kukulcán is at Chichén Itzá. For the ancient Mayas, Kukulkán was a holy place. People made **pilgrimages** to the pyramid every year.

There are two days every year when night and day are of equal length. These two days are special at Chichén Itzá. On these days, the sun makes seven triangles of shade on the steps of the pyramid. As the sun sets, the triangles get longer. The light and shadows look like a giant snake sliding down the steps.

# Vocabulary Workout

▶ **Read the titles at the top of the columns. Then read the terms in the list. Place each term in the best column.**

civilization        ancestors        astronomers
pyramid        pilgrimage

| Words That Name a Person or Group of People | Words Related to Mayan Religion |
|---|---|
|  |  |
|  |  |
|  |  |

▶ **Write a sentence of your own for each word in the word bank. The sentences do not need to be related.**

**Word Bank**
civilization
ancestors
astronomers
pyramid
pilgrimage

_____

_____

_____

_____

_____

_____

_____

_____

_____

_____

_____

_____ Workout Score (number of correct answers, from columns only)

▶ **Use the word bank to find the best word for each clue.**
**Then write the words in the puzzle.**

**ACROSS**

3. Kukulcán is one of these
4. The ancient Mayas are an example of this
5. People who study things in space

**DOWN**

1. Journey to a holy place
2. Family members who came before us

**Word Bank**
civilization
ancestors
astronomers
pyramid
pilgrimage

_____ Workout Score (number of correct answers, p. 91)

_____ Cooldown Score (number of correct answers, this page)

[    ] Add the two numbers for your Lesson 21 score.

Write the total score on page 133 next to "Lesson 21."

**Vocabulary Stretches**

▶ **Read about the social studies words related to ancient Greece.**

**political science** *(pə lit′i kəl  sī′əns)* adjective + noun
**Political science** is the study of how governments work.
A *government* is a set of leaders and the laws they use.
Cities and countries have governments.

**democratic** *(dem′ə krat′ik)* adjective
The word *democracy* comes from two Greek words.
The word *democracy* means "government by the people."
The people help to choose their leaders in a **democratic** government.
The leaders then make the laws of the democratic government.

**scientific method** *(sī′ən tif′ik  meth′əd)* adjective + noun
The **scientific method** is a process. The process has clear steps.
A man from ancient Greece named Aristotle wrote down these steps.
Today, you use the scientific method to study things and to solve problems.

**constitution** *(kon′stə too′shən)* noun
A **constitution** tells how the laws of a country work.
A constitution is in writing. A constitution is important to a government.

**pentathlon** *(pen tath′lən)* noun
A **pentathlon** was a major sporting event in ancient Greece.
There are five running and throwing events in a pentathlon.

One of the events in the **pentathlon** was the discus throw. Greek artist Myron of Athens made this sculpture over 600 years ago.

# Vocabulary Workout

▶ **Read the article to find out how the ancient Greeks have affected our lives today.**

## Key Players Encyclopedia

### Thank Goodness for the Greeks!

Greek civilization reached its high point about 2,500 years ago. Many good things in our lives came from the ancient Greeks. For example, the Greeks invented the **democratic** form of government. The Greek word for *democracy* means "government by the people." A Greek man named Plato wrote the first book on **political science.** That's the study of how governments work. Another Greek man, Solon, wrote down the laws of the Greeks. He called them a **constitution**, or "a set of rules for governing."

Aristotle

Aristotle was another great Greek thinker. He helped to develop the **scientific method.** You use this process in science class. It helps scientists study things and solve problems.

The Greeks also invented the Olympics. The **pentathlon** had five running and throwing events. The winner of the pentathlon was the best athlete. Olympic athletes were heroes back then, just as they are today.

Thank goodness for the Greeks!

# Vocabulary Workout

**Help Marta write a postcard. Use the words in the word bank to fill in the blanks.**

Dear Rafael,

We're on vacation in Greece! Today I learned that the _____ form of government started here. I saw some of the laws of ancient Greece. A man named Solon wrote them down. The laws are called a _____. Being here makes me want to know more about how governments work. I plan to study _____ in college.

I also learned that the first person to write down the _____ was Aristotle. He was also a Greek.

Yesterday, we saw where the first Olympics were held. A big part of the Greek Olympics was called the _____. The athletes participated in five running and throwing events. The ancient Greeks took care of their minds and their bodies!

See you soon.

Marta

Rafael Tapia

347 Main Street

Hometown, USA

_____ Workout Score (number of correct answers)

# Vocabulary Cooldown

▶ **Read the words in the word bank. Then find the words in the puzzle and circle them. Words can go up, down, across, or diagonally.**

| a | q | t | g | r | c | i | w | a | d | y | n | t | c | y |
|---|---|---|---|---|---|---|---|---|---|---|---|---|---|---|
| e | p | e | n | t | a | t | h | l | o | n | r | p | b | n |
| b | i | n | a | r | u | i | v | a | h | e | o | t | e | y |
| o | i | d | o | p | l | o | o | i | t | l | e | n | o | r |
| c | q | u | e | v | b | l | e | l | e | o | c | p | n | d |
| b | o | n | a | m | u | i | v | t | m | e | n | t | o | y |
| w | q | n | i | m | o | l | i | n | c | o | e | p | w | p |
| b | i | n | s | r | u | c | v | a | i | d | i | t | q | y |
| i | t | o | p | t | o | o | r | t | f | p | c | o | l | r |
| u | l | u | w | i | d | l | e | a | i | o | s | p | w | d |
| e | q | p | i | v | a | t | q | n | t | o | l | p | b | c |
| b | i | t | a | r | u | o | u | a | n | i | a | t | o | m |
| z | f | u | d | v | t | p | y | t | e | o | c | p | y | c |
| b | i | n | a | r | t | i | v | a | i | v | i | t | o | p |
| i | t | o | p | i | o | o | i | t | c | p | t | o | l | r |
| r | q | u | l | s | b | i | t | p | s | o | i | w | i | d |
| e | q | o | i | v | a | l | h | n | t | o | l | p | t | c |
| e | c | o | n | s | t | i | t | u | t | i | o | n | e | f |
| q | d | t | a | r | h | i | v | a | l | a | p | t | b | y |

**Word Bank**
constitution
political science
scientific method
democratic
pentathlon

_____ Workout Score (number of correct answers, p. 95)

_____ Cooldown Score (number of correct answers, this page)

☐ Add the two numbers for your Lesson 22 score.

**Write the total score on page 133 next to "Lesson 22."**

# Vocabulary Stretches

▶ **Read about the social studies words related to the Roman Empire.**

**emperor** *(em′pər ər)* noun
An **emperor** is a ruler. An emperor rules an *empire*.
A country becomes an empire when it takes over other countries.
Augustus was the first emperor of Rome.
The Roman Empire came after the Greek civilization.

**republic** *(ri pub′lik)* noun
A **republic** is a form of government.
In a republic, the people choose leaders to represent them.
The leaders they choose rule the country.
At first, Rome was a republic. Then it was an *empire*.

**forum** *(fôr′əm)* noun
A **forum** is a meeting place for discussions. There was a forum in Rome.
At a forum, people talk about issues that are important to the community.

**census** *(sen′səs)* noun
In a **census,** a government counts all the people.
A census tells how many people are in a city or country.

**legionaries** *(lē′jə när′ēz)* noun
**Legionaries** were soldiers. A *legion* is a division of an army.
A legion is made up of 5,000 legionaries. Legionaries lived in ancient Rome.

A drawing of a
Roman **legionary**

# Vocabulary Workout

▶ **Read how an emperor ruled long ago.**

## Augustus and Ancient Rome

Augustus was the first **emperor** of Rome, in ancient Italy, about 2,000 years ago. He used some ideas from the Roman **Republic,** which began about 500 years earlier. For example, Augustus encouraged Rome's leaders to meet at the Roman **Forum** and share their views. He also took a **census** every few years. This count of citizens helped him decide how much tax money everyone would pay.

Bust of **Emperor** Augustus

Augustus was in command of thousands of **legionaries.** However, he did not use them for war. During his rule, there was peace.

 # Vocabulary Workout

▷ **R**ead the titles at the top of the columns. Then read the terms in the list. Place each term in the best column.

emperor          legionaries          forum
republic         census

| Roman Things | Roman People |
|--------------|--------------|
|              |              |
|              |              |
|              |              |

▷ **W**rite a sentence of your own for each word in the word bank. The sentences do not need to be related.

**Word Bank**
legionaries
census
forum
republic
emperor

_____

_____

_____

_____

_____

_____

_____

_____

_____

_____

_____

_____ Workout Score (number of correct answers, from columns only)

# Vocabulary Cooldown

▶ **Use the word bank to find the best word for each clue. Then write the words in the puzzle.**

**ACROSS**

3. The type of ruler that Augustus was

4. A count of the population

5. Roman soldiers

**DOWN**

1. A government in which citizens choose their leaders

2. A meeting place for talking about issues

**Word Bank**
emperor
republic
census
forum
legionaries

_____ Workout Score (number of correct answers, p. 99)

_____ Cooldown Score (number of correct answers, this page)

[   ] Add the two numbers for your Lesson 23 score.

Write the total score on page 133 next to "Lesson 23."

Vocabulary Stretches

▶ **Read about the social studies words related to the Middle Ages.**

**lords** *(lôrds)* noun
**Lords** were men who lived during the *Middle Ages.*
The *Middle Ages* came after the Roman Empire in Europe.
Lords owned large stretches of land.

**serfs** *(surfs)* noun
**Serfs** were people who lived during the Middle Ages.
Serfs worked on the lords' land. They were not free.
Serfs could not leave the land they worked on.

**feudalism** *(fūd´əl iz´əm)* noun
**Feudalism** was the system of government in the Middle Ages.
Under feudalism, kings gave land to lords.
In return, lords fought for their king.

**castle** *(kas´əl)* noun
A **castle** is a huge stone house from the Middle Ages.
A castle protects its owner from attack.
Kings and lords often owned castles.

**knights** *(nīts)* noun
**Knights** were warriors on horseback.
Lords hired knights to fight for them.

A **castle** from the Middle Ages

 # Vocabulary Workout

Read this imaginary letter from one lord to another during the Middle Ages.

Dear Lord Charles,

I do believe that **feudalism** is a good type of goverment for us.

The king rules in his **castle** and we get our own land!

I am not worried about my land. I have hired several **knights.** They will ride out every day to watch over it.

Everyone can see that the democratic ideas of the Greeks were wrong! We **lords** know how to take care of the people. They would not know how to use power. Besides, we need **serfs** to work the land.

Good health to you, Lord Charles!

Sincerely,

Lord Henry

A **knight** on horseback

 # Vocabulary Workout

▶ **Help Lord Charles write back to Lord Henry. Underline the correct word in each pair of parentheses.**

Dear Lord Henry,

One of my (castles, knights) just rushed up on horseback to bring me your letter. It was good to hear from you! I agree with everything you say. The democratic ideas of the Greeks are not useful to us. I am a (knight, lord) and so are you. We need the (serfs, knights) to work our land. I want to keep living in a (castle, feudalism).

I do hope that (lords, feudalism) will always be our form of government. It's perfect for us!

My best wishes to you and your family!

Sincerely yours,

Lord Charles

_____ Workout Score (number of correct answers)

# Vocabulary Cooldown

▶ **Unscramble the letters below to form the words in the word bank. Put only one letter in each box.**

1. r e s s f

   ☐☐☐☐☐

2. l a d m i s u f e

   ☐☐☐☐☐☐☐☐☐

3. s e l t a c

   ☐☐☐☐☐☐

4. h n i t g s k

   ☐☐☐☐☐☐☐

5. s o l d r

   ☐☐☐☐☐

_____ Workout Score (number of correct answers, p. 103)

_____ Cooldown Score (number of correct answers, this page)

☐ Add the two numbers for your Lesson 24 score.

Write the total score on page 133 next to "Lesson 24."

Vocabulary Stretches

▶ **Read about the social studies words related to the first European people in the Americas.**

**conquistadores** *(kōn kēst'ə dô´res)* noun
   The Spanish word *conquistadores* means "conquerors."
   Conquerors rule another civilization by force.
   The **conquistadores** sailed from Spain to the continents of
     North America and South America.
   Different conquistadores ruled different civilizations by force.

**colonize** *(kol'ə nīz')* verb
   To **colonize** is to start settlements or towns in a new land.
   These settlements are called *colonies*.

**colonists** *(kol'ə nists)* noun
   **Colonists** are people who live in colonies.
   Colonists and colonies are ruled by other countries.

**revolution** *(rev'ə lōo´shən)* noun
   In a **revolution,** the people remove their own government by force.
   After a revolution, the people make a new government.

**tyranny** *(tir'ə nē)* noun
   **Tyranny** is an unjust or unfair use of power.
   Tyranny is also total control over a country or a people.

Ponce de León was a Spanish
explorer and **conquistador.**
He conquered the island that is
now called Puerto Rico. He also
explored what is now Florida.

# Vocabulary Workout

▶ **Read the passage below.**

## Conquistadores and Colonists Go to the Americas

People in Europe did not know about the continents of North America and South America. Christopher Columbus thought he was going to India when he sailed from Spain. Instead, he landed on an island in the Americas. On the island, Columbus met the Taino people.

About 25 years later, Spain sent *conquistadores* to the Americas. They conquered the "Indian" civilizations. They killed many people and destroyed cities. Then, Spain and other countries in Europe **colonized** parts of the Americas. They sent **colonists** to set up colonies.

After many years, some colonists wanted their own governments. They no longer wanted to be under the **tyranny** of kings in Europe. A group of colonists in North America lead a **revolution** against England. They set up a new country called the United States of America. Several years later, colonists in Mexico and South America had revolutions against Spain and Portugal. They also formed new countries.

 **Vocabulary Workout**

▶ **Put these vocabulary words from the last 5 lessons in their time groups.**

conquistadores          legionaries          census          castle
pyramid                 pentathlon           lords           knights
forum                   feudalism            revolution      democracy
astronomers             colonists

| Ancient Mayan Civilization | Greek Civilization | Roman Civilization | The Middle Ages | "Conquistadores and Colonists Go to the Americas" |
|---|---|---|---|---|
|  |  |  |  |  |
|  |  |  |  |  |
|  |  |  |  |  |
|  |  |  |  |  |

▶ **Write a sentence of your own for each word in the word bank. The sentences do not need to be related.**

**Word Bank**
conquistadores
tyranny
colonize
revolution
colonists

_____

_____

_____

_____

_____

_____

_____

_____

_____

_____ Workout Score (number of correct answers, from columns only)

# Vocabulary Cooldown

▶ **Read the words in the word bank. Then find them in the puzzle and circle them. Words can go up, down, across, or diagonally.**

| b | i | t | a | r | u | i | c | n | n | i | s | t | s | d |
|---|---|---|---|---|---|---|---|---|---|---|---|---|---|---|
| a | q | t | g | r | c | i | o | t | l | y | n | n | c | n |
| q | i | s | t | r | h | i | c | a | y | a | n | t | b | y |
| e | d | a | y | f | u | q | o | n | c | r | r | p | i | c |
| b | i | n | a | r | u | i | z | a | o | e | a | t | o | y |
| n | n | t | e | q | l | o | c | o | l | o | p | n | o | r |
| n | q | o | z | e | d | l | m | n | o | o | q | p | n | c |
| y | q | n | i | v | b | l | e | l | n | u | r | u | i | y |
| t | c | o | l | o | n | i | z | e | i | e | n | t | o | y |
| n | q | i | i | l | a | l | q | s | s | o | r | u | i | o |
| n | i | t | a | u | u | i | t | a | t | d | n | l | z | e |
| i | t | u | o | l | o | a | s | t | s | p | q | o | e | o |
| r | l | l | v | i | d | n | e | t | b | o | r | v | o | c |
| y | q | o | e | o | a | l | e | o | l | o | c | p | n | n |
| t | i | v | r | r | u | n | z | e | l | h | n | t | o | d |
| z | f | e | y | v | t | l | n | s | t | s | r | p | d | c |
| b | s | r | a | q | u | m | t | y | a | n | a | n | a | y |
| i | t | o | p | l | i | o | n | t | o | p | l | o | k | r |

**Word Bank**

conquistadores
tyranny
colonize
revolution
colonists

---

_____ Workout Score (number of correct answers, p. 107)

_____ Cooldown Score (number of correct answers, this page)

☐ Add the two numbers for your Lesson 25 score.

Write the total score on page 133 next to "Lesson 25."

▶ **Underline the correct word in each set of parentheses.**

### Freedom in the Americas

In the Americas, different people have wanted freedom from different things. The (conquistadores, colonists) came to the Americas from Spain. They wanted "freedom" to rule other civilizations. The colonists wanted freedom from their rulers far away. The colonists accused these rulers of (revolution, tyranny). Some colonists started a (revolution, tyranny) to form a new country. Meanwhile, the Native Americans wanted the freedom to live on the land. When people came to (colonize, Conquistadores) the Americas, they pushed Native Americans off the land. At the same time, enslaved people wanted freedom from the (revolution, colonists) themselves.

They wanted the most basic freedom, freedom from slavery.

▶ **Read the ad. Fill in the blanks with the words from the list.**

**Word Bank**

astronomers
pyramid
pilgrimage
civilization
ancestors

### Pilgrimage to Chichén Itzá

Next week, people from around the world will travel to Chichén Itzá, Mexico. They will make a _____.

The _____ of many people made the same trip thousands of years ago. See the giant _____ of Kukulcán!

Learn how _____ designed the pyramid. You'll be amazed at what you see come down the steps. Don't miss the chance to experience this part of Mayan _____.

▶ **Read the titles at the top of the columns. Then read the terms in the list. Place each term in the best column.**

| democratic | knights | republic | serfs |
|---|---|---|---|
| feudalism | lords | legionaries | |

| People Who Serve Under an Emperor or King | Kinds of Government |
|---|---|
| | |
| | |
| | |
| | |

▶ **Write a sentence of your own for each word or term in the list. The sentences do not need to be related.**

| constitution | scientific method | political science | castle |
|---|---|---|---|
| pentathlon | emperor | forum | census |

_____

_____

_____

_____

_____

_____

_____

_____

_____

# Vocabulary Stretches

▶ **Read about the social studies words related to workers and factories in the United States.**

**immigrants** *(im´ə grənts)* noun
**Immigrants** are people who go to live in another country.

**tenements** *(ten´ə mənts)* noun
**Tenements** were a kind of housing for workers in cities.
Tenements were often crowded and unsafe.
Many immigrants lived in tenements.

**urbanization** *(ər bə nə zā´shən)* noun
**Urbanization** is the growth of cities.
People moving from farms and small towns into cities is called urbanization.

**factory system** *(fak´tər ē sis´təm)* adjective + noun
The **factory system** is a way to make goods.
The factory system puts many workers and machines together in one place.
After the factory system started, many workers no longer worked at home.

**assembly line** *(ə sem´blē līn)* adjective + noun
An **assembly line** is a line of machines and people.
An assembly line is often a part of a factory system.
On an assembly line, each worker does one job over and over.
The worker's job is to add one part to a product.

Workers at this factory in Connecticut wound silk thread onto spools all day.

# Vocabulary Workout

▶ **Read this article about Cesar Chavez.**

## Key Players Encyclopedia

### Cesar Chavez

At age ten, Cesar Chavez was already working. His mother and father were **immigrants** from Mexico. They worked on other people's farms. With increased **urbanization** in the United States, many American farm workers moved to the cities. They often became part of the **factory system** and worked on **assembly lines.** Farm workers were then hired from Mexico. But the workers were not treated fairly. They worked long hours in the hot sun. Their pay was very low. Their living conditions were often worse than in the **tenements** of the city.

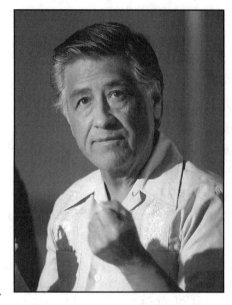

In 1962, Cesar Chavez created a union for farm workers. Through this union, farm workers made a plan. They went on *strike.* They announced they would all stop working unless they got better pay and conditions. The union became the UFW, the United Farm Workers. It has helped improve the lives of thousands of people.

> *"We are ready to give up everything—even our lives—in our struggle for justice."*
>
> Cesar Chavez
> (1927–1993)

# Vocabulary Workout

▶ **Read this article about city factory workers in 1911. Use the words in the word bank to complete it.**

## April 28, 1911
## Terrible Fire in Factory

Today, 146 people died in a factory fire. They were locked inside the building and could not escape the fire.

The Triangle Shirtwaist Factory kept all the machines and all the workers in the same area. The workers were not all in a row on an _____, but they were all in the same area. The owners didn't trust the workers. They locked most of the doors to keep workers from leaving early. Then the fire started.

Many workers who died were _____ from other countries. They lived in _____. Now workers are getting together to push for better fire laws. In these days of _____, cities are growing fast. We need the _____ to provide goods for everyone, but we have to make it safe.

**Word Bank**
factory system
tenements
immigrants
assembly line
urbanization

_____ Workout Score (number of correct answers)

# Vocabulary Cooldown

▶ **Read the words in the word bank. Then find them in the puzzle and circle them. Words can go up, down, across, or diagonally.**

| u | s | t | a | r | u | i | v | a | z | a | u | t | e | y |
|---|---|---|---|---|---|---|---|---|---|---|---|---|---|---|
| r | d | s | i | f | a | c | o | r | y | o | r | p | i | t |
| b | i | n | a | r | u | i | t | a | z | i | b | t | e | t |
| f | i | t | m | p | r | o | s | i | t | o | a | n | o | o |
| a | s | s | e | m | b | l | y | l | i | n | e | p | i | r |
| i | q | u | t | g | a | l | s | l | t | m | r | p | i | y |
| z | i | n | s | i | n | l | y | a | e | i | m | t | o | s |
| w | q | v | y | m | i | l | t | n | t | t | e | m | r | p |
| b | i | n | s | m | z | a | t | l | l | i | t | t | o | s |
| i | t | o | y | i | a | s | n | t | i | z | s | s | a | t |
| u | l | s | r | g | t | z | e | t | n | o | y | n | m | o |
| r | q | p | o | v | i | t | s | y | s | m | r | p | i | r |
| b | r | t | t | r | o | i | e | t | e | m | o | l | o | h |
| a | f | u | c | v | n | l | m | n | t | o | t | p | i | s |
| s | t | n | a | r | g | i | m | m | i | v | n | t | o | y |
| i | t | r | f | l | o | o | e | t | o | p | e | o | l | s |
| r | q | u | r | s | e | m | b | l | t | r | m | p | n | t |

**Word Bank**
immigrants
tenements
urbanization
factory system
assembly line

---

_____ Workout Score (number of correct answers, p. 113)

_____ Cooldown Score (number of correct answers, this page)

[ ] Add the two numbers for your Lesson 26 score.

Write the total score on page 133 next to "Lesson 26."

# Vocabulary Stretches

▶ **Read about the social studies words related to World War I.**

**armaments** *(arʹmə mənts)* noun
**Armaments** are weapons used for war.
Armaments also include boats and planes used in war.

**artillery** *(ar tilʹər ē)* noun
**Artillery** is a type of weapon for war.
Artillery includes guns that are too big for one person to carry.
Artillery guns are mounted on "legs."
In World War I, the United States and several countries
in Europe fought Germany.
The armaments of World War I included artillery.

**armistice** *(arʹmi stis)* noun
An **armistice** is an agreement to end a war.
Armistice Day marked the end of World War I on November 11, 1918.
Today, we celebrate Armistice Day as Veterans Day.

**civilians** *(si vilʹyənz)* noun
**Civilians** are people who are not soldiers.

**trench warfare** *(trenchʹ wôrʹfār)* noun + noun
**Trench warfare** is a form of fighting in a war.
In trench warfare, enemies fight each other from long ditches.
Trench warfare was used in World War I.

On the next page, read about
African American heroes from the
first World War. Here they march in
a parade in New York in 1916.

# Vocabulary Workout

▶ **Read Charise's letter to a military museum.**

Atlanta, Georgia
March 7, 2006

New York Military Museum
1000 Military St.
New York, NY

Dear Friends:

I would like to know more about my great-grandfather, John Abrahams. He served in World War I in France. His group of soldiers was called the 369th Regiment. All the soldiers were African Americans. John's letters say that he knew a lot about guns and other kinds of **armaments**. He was an expert on **artillery,** or mounted guns. His letters described lying in a long ditch behind the artillery. He spent many months in **trench warfare**. Unfortunately, he didn't live to see the end of the war. He died before the **armistice** was signed in 1918.

None of his great-grandchildren are in the military. We are all **civilians**. However, we are interested in his military experience.

Sincerely,

Charise Abrahams

# Vocabulary Workout

**Help someone from the New York Military Museum write a letter back to Charise. Use the words in the word bank to fill in the blanks.**

**Word Bank**

artillery
armistice
trench warfare
civilian
armaments

Dear Ms. Abrahams,

Like you, I am not in the military. I am a _____.
However, I have studied a lot about weapons of war, also called
_____, from World War I. Your
great-grandfather John is in our museum. Another soldier wrote about him in
a diary. John spent more than a year firing _____ from
ditches. This kind of fighting, known as _____,
was extremely difficult. John died during a long battle against the Germans.
He would not give up his position or his artillery.

I am sorry John did not live
to see the _____
of 1918. That was the end of
the war. Everyone in the 369th
Regiment received a medal
of honor from France. Here
is a picture of the regiment
returning from France in 1919.

Sincerely,

William Johnson

_____ Workout Score (number of correct answers)

 **Vocabulary Cooldown**

▶ **Unscramble the letters below to form the words in the word bank. Put only one letter in each box.**

**1.** m a m e r t a n s

<br>

**2.** l e r y i l r a t

<br>

**3.** r a m i t s c e i

<br>

**4.** n e r t h c   f e r a w r a

<br>

**5.** l i a v i n i s c

<br>

**Word Bank**

artillery
armistice
trench warfare
civilians
armaments

_____ Workout Score (number of correct answers, p. 117)

_____ Cooldown Score (number of correct answers, this page)

[ ] Add the two numbers for your Lesson 27 score.

**Write the total score on page 133 next to "Lesson 27,"**

# Social Studies

## Vocabulary Stretches

▶ **Read about the social studies words related to World War II and the Holocaust.**

**Nazis** *(not´sēz)* noun
The **Nazis** were members of Germany's National Socialist Party.
The Nazis took power in 1933. Adolf Hitler was the leader of the Nazis.
Under the Nazis, Germany invaded other countries in Europe.
These invasions caused the beginning of World War II.

**genocide** *(jen´ə sīd´)* noun
**Genocide** is an effort to murder an entire people and destroy their culture.
Genocide is a crime of great violence and hatred.

**Holocaust** *(Hol´ə kôst´)* noun
**Holocaust** is great destruction and loss of life, usually by fire.
The Nazis carried out genocide through the Holocaust.
In the Holocaust, the Nazis killed more than 6 million Jewish people.
The Nazis killed other civilians in the Holocaust, as well.

**dictator** *(dik´tā´ tər)* noun
A **dictator** is a type of ruler. Hitler was a dictator.
A dictator has all the power in a government. A dictator often rules unjustly.

**concentration camps** *(kon´sən trā´shən  kamps´)* adjective + noun
**Concentration camps** are huge prison camps.
Governments hold their enemies in concentration camps.
The conditions in concentration camps are extremely bad.
The Nazis put millions of Jews and other people in concentration camps.

**Nazi** flags in a history museum

# Vocabulary Workout

▶ **Read this article about Anne Frank.**

## Key Players Encyclopedia

### Anne Frank (1929–1945)

Anne Frank was a young German Jewish girl during World War II. The **Nazis** and their **dictator,** Adolf Hitler, were in power. They were carrying out a program of **genocide** against Jewish people and others. During the **Holocaust,** the Nazis killed more than 6 million Jewish people just because they were Jews.

In 1933, Anne's family fled the Nazis in Germany and settled in The Netherlands. Then Germany gained control of The Netherlands. Anne's family hid from the Nazis in an attic. Every day, Anne wrote down her thoughts and feelings in her diary. After 25 months, the Nazis found Anne and her family. The Nazis took them to **concentration camps.** Anne got sick and died in the concentration camp. She was only 15 years old.

After the war was over, Anne's diary was found in the attic where she had lived in hiding. Since then, millions of people all over the world have read Anne's words.

> *"I still believe that people are really good at heart."*
>
> *Anne Frank*
> *(1929–1945)*

 **Vocabulary Workout**

▶ **Help Hannah write an e-mail to Manuel. Underline the correct word in each pair of parentheses.**

TO:        Manuel

FROM:     Hannah

SUBJECT:  Holocaust Museum

   I just went to a museum about the Nazis and the _____.

The museum had pictures of Hitler. He was the _____

of Germany. He and the _____ tried to destroy the

entire Jewish people. They were guilty of _____.

The Nazis put people in _____. They burned the

bodies of millions of people in huge ovens! I need to talk to you more about

what I saw there.

Hannah

# Vocabulary Cooldown

▶ **Use the word bank to complete each sentence below. Then write the words in the puzzle.**

ACROSS

**4.** The people who planned the Holocaust

**5.** Places where the Nazis put prisoners

DOWN

**1.** An example of genocide

**2.** A leader with total power

**3.** A crime against a whole people

**Word Bank**
Nazis
concentration camps
dictator
genocide
Holocaust

_____ Workout Score (number of correct answers, p. 121)

_____ Cooldown Score (number of correct answers, this page)

[ ] Add the two numbers for your Lesson 28 score.

Write the total score on page 133 next to "Lesson 28."

**Vocabulary Stretches**

▶ **Read about the social studies words related to the Cold War.**

**satellite nations** *(sat′əl īt′ nā′shəns)* noun + noun
**Satellite nations** are countries.
Satellite nations are controlled by a stronger country.

**aggression** *(ə gresh′ən)* noun
**Aggression** is attacking first.
Aggression is warlike action.

**Cold War** *(kōld wôr)* adjective + noun
The **Cold War** started after World War II.
The Cold War was between the United States and the *Soviet Union.*
The Soviet Union was a large country made up of Russia and other republics.
In the Cold War, the United States and the Soviet Union did not fight each
  other directly.

**autonomous** *(ô ton′ə məs)* noun
Being **autonomous** means being able to make decisions for yourself.
A person or group can be autonomous from a larger group.
Countries that can govern themselves are called autonomous.

**sovereign** *(sov′rən)* noun
A **sovereign** country is autonomous and governs itself.
A sovereign country is independent from other countries.
A sovereign country makes decisions about its people for itself.

Soviet leader Mikhail
Gorbachev and U.S. President
Ronald Reagan met in 1985.
This meeting helped to end
the **Cold War.**

# Vocabulary Workout

▶ **Read this article about the Cold War.**

## The Cold War

During World War II, the United States fought against the Nazis. So did the Soviet Union. Millions of people from the Soviet Union died fighting the Nazis. However, after the war, the United States and the Soviet Union became enemies. The two countries had totally different types of government. They never declared war on each other. However, their unfriendly relationship was called the **Cold War.**

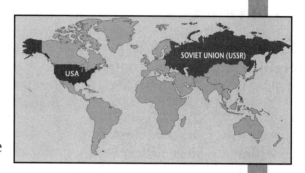

First the United States and then the Soviet Union developed nuclear bombs. All of the bombs together were powerful enough to destroy the world. Neither country started a nuclear war. However, both countries used military **aggression** against smaller countries. Many of these small countries were not treated as **sovereign** countries. They could not always act in an **autonomous** way.

By 1991, 16 republics inside the Soviet Union had become independent. Today the Soviet Union no longer exists as one country. Its **satellite nations,** such as Lithuania, are now independent. People in the United States and the former Soviet Union have a more friendly relationship. They have even destroyed some of their nuclear bombs. The Cold War is over.

 **Vocabulary Workout**

▶ **Read the titles at the top of the columns. Then read the terms in the list. Place each term in the best column.**

Cold War          aggression          sovereign
autonomous        satellite nations

| Words That Describe an Independent Country | Words About Relationships Between Countries |
|---|---|
|  |  |
|  |  |
|  |  |

▶ **Write a sentence of your own for each word or term in the word bank. The sentences do not need to be related.**

**Word Bank**

Cold War

aggression

satellite nations

sovereign

autonomous

_____

_____

_____

_____

_____

_____

_____

_____

_____

_____

_____ Workout Score (number of correct answers, from columns only)

# Vocabulary Cooldown

▶ **Unscramble the letters below to form the words in the word bank. Put only one letter in each box.**

**1.** g r e n i v o s e

[ ][ ][ ][ ][ ][ ][ ][ ][ ]

**Word Bank**

Cold War

aggression

satellite nations

sovereign

autonomous

**2.** n o t a u m o s o u

[ ][ ][ ][ ][ ][ ][ ][ ][ ][ ]

**3.** g e r a g s i n o s

[ ][ ][ ][ ][ ][ ][ ][ ][ ][ ]

**4.** d c l o   a r w

[ ][ ][ ][ ]   [ ][ ][ ]

**5.** t i l e s e l t a   i n o t a n s

[ ][ ][ ][ ][ ][ ][ ][ ][ ]   [ ][ ][ ][ ][ ][ ][ ]

_____ Workout Score (number of correct answers, p. 125)

_____ Cooldown Score (number of correct answers, this page)

[ ] Add the two numbers for your Lesson 29 score.

Write the total score on page 133 next to "Lesson 29."

# Vocabulary Stretches

▶ **Read about the social studies words related to developing nations of today.**

**developing nations** *(di vel´əp ing  nā´shəns)*  adjective + noun
The **developing nations** of today depend mainly on farming.
Developing nations do not have many factories.
*Developed* nations have great wealth and produce lots of goods.
Developing nations are working to produce more goods and gain wealth.

**cash crops** *(kash´ krops´)*  noun + noun
**Cash crops** are crops that are grown and sold in the market.
Cash crops are also nonfood crops such as cotton.

**subsistence farmers** *(səb sis´təns  far´mərs)*  adjective + noun
**Subsistence farmers** are people who grow food.
Subsistence farmers grow only enough food for their own use.
Subsistence farmers do not grow cash crops.

**communicable diseases** *(kə mū´ni kə bəl  di zēz´es)*  adjective + noun
**Communicable diseases** are illnesses that one person can give to another person.
Many people in developing nations suffer from communicable diseases.
An example of a communicable disease is chicken pox.

**extended families** *(iks ten´did  fam´ə lēs)*  adjective + noun
**Extended families** include grandparents, cousins, and others.
Members of extended families often live in the same house.

A **subsistence farmer** in Guatemala hoes his crops.

▶ **Read this press release about an evening with Rigoberta Menchú.**

# An Evening with Rigoberta Menchú

Come hear Rigoberta Menchú speak about **developing nations.** Menchú is a Mayan woman from Guatemala. Many people there are farmers. Some of them grow **cash crops** to sell. Others are **subsistence farmers.** In bad years, these farmers often do not have enough food to eat. Many people also suffer from **communicable diseases.**

As a young woman, Rigoberta Menchú wanted to help the people of Guatemala. She joined a union with many farmers in it. The government did not like this group. Everyone in the union was in danger. Their **extended families** were in danger, too. Menchú's father, brother, and mother were all killed by the army of Guatemala.

In 1981, Menchú fled Guatemala. She spoke about human rights in other countries. She spoke about the need for peace and development. She spoke about the rights of Mayas and other Native Americans. In 1992, she won the Nobel Peace Prize. Come hear her speak!

# Vocabulary Workout

▶ **Read the titles at the top of the columns. Then read the terms in the list. Place each term in the best column.**

developing nations          cash crops              extended families
communicable diseases       subsistence farmers

| Groups of People | Things |
|---|---|
|  |  |
|  |  |
|  |  |

▶ **Write a sentence of your own for each word or term in the word bank. The sentences do not need to be related.**

_____

_____

_____

_____

_____

_____

_____

_____

_____

_____

**Word Bank**

communicable
  diseases
cash crops
extended families
subsistence farmers
developing nations

_____ Workout Score (number of correct answers, for columns only)

# Vocabulary Cooldown

▶ **Read the words in the word bank. Then find them in the puzzle and circle them. Words can go up, down, across, or diagonally.**

| z | f | s | a | v | e | l | y | n | t | o | r | s | i | c |
|---|---|---|---|---|---|---|---|---|---|---|---|---|---|---|
| i | s | o | p | l | e | o | i | t | o | p | l | e | l | r |
| e | n | s | i | f | a | l | o | n | t | o | r | s | e | c |
| b | o | u | r | a | i | e | v | p | l | e | n | a | x | a |
| o | i | b | o | r | l | o | o | i | t | x | p | e | t | m |
| c | t | s | p | m | d | l | m | n | f | t | r | s | e | i |
| c | a | i | i | u | b | l | e | g | t | e | r | i | x | l |
| b | n | s | a | m | u | q | l | r | l | n | n | d | d | s |
| w | g | t | h | m | g | l | d | t | t | d | r | e | e | c |
| b | n | e | a | c | u | m | v | a | l | e | n | l | d | h |
| u | i | n | i | r | l | e | t | b | d | r | b | f | c |  |
| e | p | c | i | v | a | o | d | n | t | f | r | a | a | d |
| b | o | e | a | r | n | i | p | i | h | a | n | c | c | y |
| b | l | f | a | r | m | i | e | s | l | m | n | i | m | p |
| i | e | a | p | c | r | o | a | t | o | i | n | n | i | r |
| e | v | r | i | v | e | c | p | n | t | l | r | u | l | c |
| b | e | m | a | r | u | e | v | e | d | i | u | m | e | h |
| a | d | e | g | s | c | r | o | a | l | e | n | m | b | r |
| r | d | r | i | s | b | i | t | p | t | s | r | o | u | c |
| q | d | s | a | r | h | e | v | e | l | a | n | c | s | m |

**Word Bank**

developing nations
cash crops
subsistence farmers
communicable diseases
extended families

_____ Workout Score (number of correct answers, p. 129)

_____ Cooldown Score (number of correct answers, this page)

[  ] Add the two numbers for your Lesson 30 score.

**Write the total score on page 133 next to "Lesson 30."**

► **Underline the correct word in each pair of parentheses.**

## Cold War Conflict

After World War II, the United States and the Soviet Union were in conflict.

They were in a (autonomous, Cold War). Both countries used military

(sovereign, aggression) against their neighbors. These small countries were

not always treated like (sovereign, Cold War) countries. They could not always act in an

(aggression, autonomous) way. Some of the countries were (satellite nations, Cold War).

► **Read this e-mail. Then fill in the blanks with the words in the box.**

**Word Bank**

cash crops
subsistence farmers
communicable diseases
extended families
developing nation

TO:     Jabril
FROM:  Pedro

Hey, Jabril. I have great news! My Mom is taking me

to visit Honduras. That's where she was born.

Honduras depends on farming. Honduras is a _____. In Honduras, many

people live with their _____. We will stay with our relatives. Last year

it didn't rain much in Honduras. That means people won't have much money. The cotton

farmers depend on selling their _____. Many farmers outside the city

grow only enough for their families. They are called _____.

My doctor will give me a shot against several _____. The shot

will protect me. I'll see you when I get back!

Pedro

# Less

▶ **Read the titles at the top of the columns. Then read the terms in the list. Place each term in the best column.**

concentration camps      urbanization      armaments
factory system           assembly line     artillery
immigrants               tenements         trench warfare

| Words Related to Cities and Factories | Words Related to War |
|---|---|
|  |  |
|  |  |
|  |  |
|  |  |
|  |  |

▶ **Write a sentence of your own for each word or term in the word bank. The sentences do not need to be related.**

armistice      civilians      genocide      Nazis      Holocaust      dictator

_____

_____

_____

_____

_____

_____

_____

_____

# Lesson Scores

Record your lesson scores below.

| SCIENCE | MATH | SOCIAL STUDIES |
|---------|------|----------------|
| Lesson 1 _____ | Lesson 11 _____ | Lesson 21 _____ |
| Lesson 2 _____ | Lesson 12 _____ | Lesson 22 _____ |
| Lesson 3 _____ | Lesson 13 _____ | Lesson 23 _____ |
| Lesson 4 _____ | Lesson 14 _____ | Lesson 24 _____ |
| Lesson 5 _____ | Lesson 15 _____ | Lesson 25 _____ |
| Lesson 6 _____ | Lesson 16 _____ | Lesson 26 _____ |
| Lesson 7 _____ | Lesson 17 _____ | Lesson 27 _____ |
| Lesson 8 _____ | Lesson 18 _____ | Lesson 28 _____ |
| Lesson 9 _____ | Lesson 19 _____ | Lesson 29 _____ |
| Lesson 10 _____ | Lesson 20 _____ | Lesson 30 _____ |
| **Total Science Score:** [ ] | **Total Math Score:** [ ] | **Total Social Studies Score:** [ ] |

**Note:** Total possible score for each subject area is 100 points.

# Assessment Scores

When your teacher gives you an assessment score, record it below.

| SCIENCE | MATH | SOCIAL STUDIES |
|---------|------|----------------|
| Lessons 1–5 _____ | Lessons 11–15 _____ | Lessons 21–25 _____ |
| Lessons 6–10 _____ | Lessons 16–20 _____ | Lessons 26–30 _____ |

# Index of Vocabulary Words

# Photo Credits